"*Guess What's Differ* [...] cal soul work."

    —Nick Olson, author of *Here's Waldo*, *The Brother We Share*, and *Afterglow*.

"With language tender in its detail and heartbreakingly sad, Triemert reflects on the loss of her parents and the adoption of her sons, building for herself 'a place where every being who lives here has been chosen, a place where everyone belongs.' *Guess What's Different* is one such place for the reader as well—a home that puts striking, moving language to those feelings of anxiety, desertion, and all things love."

    —Susan L. Leary,
author of *Contraband Paradise*

"*Guess What's Different* is like a magic trick—building itself up out of emptiness; balancing one loss against another; and adding in precise amounts of beauty, humor, and honesty until Triemert has conjured from the remnants an intimate portrait of what it truly means to be a family, rough edges and all."

    —Jenniey Tallman

Guess What's Different

Essays by Susan Triemert

Malarkey Books

Published May 2022 by Malarkey Books
Print ISBN: 978-1-0879-3470-9
Ebook available at publisher's website
www.malarkeybooks.com

Cover design and typesetting by Alan Good

To my mother, whose imprint has been made on so many of these pages; my sister, who lived so many of these moments alongside me; to John, who supported my writing so very much; and to my sons, Mitch and Jack, who make it all worthwhile.

You're a High Flying Flag

You find yourself in the back of an ambulance, a slow, no-sirens, no-rushing-whatsoever type of ambulance. It dawns on you, you've seen vehicles like this and wondered why they hadn't been going faster. Ambulances are for emergencies, right? You realize that yours, the one you're strapped into, has two jobs: to carry you from one hospital to another. And to keep you safe—from yourself. Perhaps others. Once strapped inside, speed is not important. Once strapped inside, safety is no longer an issue.

Even as you half-sit, half-lean against the cot, squeezed between two paramedics—if it hadn't been such a depressing day you might have appreciated how handsome they both were—you feel a strong urge to report back to your sister and close friends that you've solved the mystery behind the slow-moving ambulance. Could they all have been driving people like you, people who had just been to the ER, people who are now headed to a psych ward? These vehicles must have other purposes, you realize, but in this moment you feel you've discovered something profound. In your case, the second hospital is over an hour away, and the drive becomes a long, drawn-out sigh. You count the barns and silos you pass, the mile markers, your breaths. Relieved those sirens are not blaring.

You tell yourself you need to remember whatever you see on this night, the night you're admitted, a hollowed-out moan of a night. It is the week of the Fourth, a Sunday evening. Most of the usual staff—as you later find out—are home with their families. Even though you are sad and scared and feel alone, you know you must remember details. You tell yourself you may need to recall them one day. You tell yourself you may never. Either way, you know you must remember.

And you want to forget so much. You want to forget about the war vet who has a train track of staples stitched across his neck—a remnant from his failed attempt to slice through skin and spine. When he's to be released the day after you arrive, his adult children and doctors decide he isn't ready for the simple reason that he refuses to lock up his firearms. From a distance you hear: "It's a free country." You are privately relieved; his slightly twisted jokes remind you of a beloved uncle's, and you need him to stay. "I'm playing here all week," he says. You watch as he throws his arms in the air, shuffles a sideways jig back into his room. In a place where everyone is sad, where laughter is hard to come by, you appreciate whatever humor and entertainment you can find.

You won't forget about the curly-haired, petite woman who tells you she's been in and out of places like this for the past ten years. Or was it twenty, she says. You confide in a kind nurse how you don't want that to be you. Randy assures you that many people come in once, for a jump start, he calls it. Most never return, he says. You desperately want to believe him. You worry that he is wrong.

Days after being admitted, you ask to change rooms—your window faces the hospital's common indoor area, with no natural light. You need sunshine. You know you can't make it through in the dark.

You're admitted in rust-colored scrubs and have nothing else to wear, so your husband heads to Target to buy clothes, safe clothing—no zippers, no strings. You recognize a woman from the ER, admitted on the same day as you, and by midweek she is still wearing those same scrubs, now rolled up to look like cargo shorts. You tell her you'll lend her a pair of black leggings. When you deliver them to her doorway, her eyes fill with tears. "This may be the nicest thing anyone has ever done for me," she says. You feel like a fraud, guilty even, knowing there are four other pairs with tags back in your room. Your room—with new pajamas, socks, sweatshirts, CDs, photos of your children, fresh flowers in a safe wooden (not glass) vase. Light.

You have a history of depression, though it was anxiety that sent you to the ER. The anxiety is more recent. Endless worry about your children, their safety, their health, yours, your future, theirs. It feels overwhelming—suffocating even. At times, unbearable.

On one visit, your husband stops at a nearby bookstore and brings back books you'd been meaning to read. Not to disrupt your exercise routine, he picks up hand weights, too. When he arrives with two bags—some people have no deliveries whatsoever—you start to believe that you are going to be okay.

You spend your wedding anniversary in the ward. You mention this to the others at dinner, and a few people chuckle. A young hospital employee who has already been admitted once this same year turns your way and tells you that you deserve another piece of chocolate cake.

"Maybe we all do. It IS the week of the Fourth," says the war vet as he thumbs the last crumb of chocolate off his plate. "If I don't, I'm going to kill myself." He laughs, exposing silver caps and nicotine stains and cake, and the rest of you can't help but join in.

Your sister makes the hour-and-a-half trip and brings soda and Tootsie Rolls and Reese's Peanut Butter Cups. Fancy soaps and lotions, too—more than you could ever need. You don't tell her about the ambulance drivers, not yet. She spends hours with you, meeting everyone you'd talked about. In the common area, you share your candy; even the nurses and social workers seem to appreciate a distraction.

You know you never want to come back, so you attend all the meetings, go to every yoga session, participate in the silly activities, like Bingo and bocce ball. And you want to forget it's the Fourth. You imagine your family hanging out at the lake, shooting off fireworks, paddling around in kayaks. You want to forget what they are doing as your group and psych patients from other floors gather around an old wooden piano. Listening to "You're a Grand Ol' Flag," you watch a young, pale man from another group drool and pretend he can fly. In your head, he becomes Flying Man. You realize your group is not the worst off. Later you eat patriotic cake: strawberry- and blueberry-covered angel food, and listen to CDs chosen by the staff—a broken record of show tunes. Again, you hear "You're a high-flying flag." For some reason, this is the only song you remember. Every time you think of it, you picture Flying Man.

You beg the staff to take your group out to the yard for an extra hour, and they do. Though not everyone wants to be outside, and that makes you sad.

You spend eight days there. You never expected it to be that long. As you leave you exchange email addresses with other patients though you know you won't keep in touch. You follow a couple people on Facebook until it all becomes too depressing, and you end up quitting Facebook altogether.

***

Once home, you wonder what happened to the newlywed with the sunken eyes who never smiled. In an oversized hospital gown, he walked the halls and spoke to no one. He refused to take off his gown. Or shower. Or eat. His wife, a kind professor, spent hours at the hospital, but ended up spending most of her time talking to you and the other women. When it was just the two of them, she'd hold his hand and hum. You wonder if another woman, a talkative female patient you liked, ended up getting her children back. She'd suck on nicotine sticks, try to settle her shaking hands, and speak about her kids. She flashed an old Christmas photo to anyone willing to look. Her new boyfriend visited daily and played Apples to Apples with the group. Although touching is not allowed, you hugged her when she left. No one said anything.

Two years later, you are back at the hospital for a different reason. You stop by the ward and wait outside. Twenty minutes tick by, then out saunters Randy, the kind nurse who'd given you hope. Seated at a nearby bench, you rise and face him.

He pivots, points. "You again." A smile flashes across his face.

You tell him how much he helped you, how you will always be grateful for his care and compassion. He thanks you, says he appreciates it. Acts as if he'd been thanked endless times, by hundreds of patients like you. Though you know he hadn't—you have met those people. People like you. Fragile people. As you walk away, you refrain from peeking through the glass window; if you recognize anyone, you know the worry will kick in: about them, yourself, your kids. By then you've forgotten *exactly* what Flying Man looks like, and this feels like an important step toward health.

You've now spent the past seven Independence Days with your family doing things you'd imagined they'd been doing. You are in therapy, medicated, you meditate, practice self-care. You wonder how many years need to pass before you can convince yourself that your time there was the jump start you needed.

A jump start. And nothing more.

Losing Her All Over Again

The night I couldn't find my mother's grave, I cried into my collar. The cemetery had grown, bloated in a way that only spirits could tolerate. Mortals, they'd have complained about the hassle, all of that dust and noise. I noticed how new stretches of road had been paved, and how fresh blades of grass had sprouted where trees had been downed. And the oaks and maples that remained had shot up even more; their encroaching branches, pressed against the sky, had formed a canopy to choke out the moon. Flattened tombstones spied through the collecting debris of leaves and twigs, erasing names, dates, any traces of existence. My mother's grave was also flat, and even though it lived in the same shadows as my father's, it had been lost. Blocked by towering tombstones, ostentatious even, as if to flash the family's wealth even in the afterlife.

To find my mother's grave, I used a mausoleum as a marker. Though more stone houses had been built, and they all looked the same. I imagined the souls locked inside yearning for the last few of their kind to join. Holding their empty breaths each time a key dug into the lock of their wrought iron door. Who had died this time, they'd say. Had they been granted a moment—time to say goodbye, to accept that this was the end? Or had life been snatched away in one lonely heartbeat?

I imagine the souls in the mausoleum that I depended on, the one I'd trusted to guide me to the grave. In a collective whisper, they'd say, *If only we could blow you a breeze, one strong enough to hold back the branches that shut out the light. Let the moon guide you to your mother.*

Second Summer

(1977) Nowhere else in the world could there be as many stars. Brilliance blurring, streaks reaching and smearing across the darkened sky. Is this what they mean by infinity? Roof to headlight, we lie across my mother's olive-green Pinto, the warm engine baking our hips, our necks, the smalls of our backs. Here in Renville, Minnesota, the farming town where my mother was raised, my sister and I point out constellations—Orion's belt, the dippers, both big and small—and create our own. A tabby playing with string, I say, then point North—a bridge lit up at night. Stargaze, starlight, stardust, utterly starstruck. So many stars.

As if driving by the rows of crops on the way here had not mesmerized us enough. The columns of soybeans and corn ticked by, lane after lane. I'd focus on the spaces, the unused soil, seeing how far each groove snaked off, hoping to catch a line that had veered, proof a farmer had made a mistake.

I shouldn't have turned to the stars and the corn—they were never the keepers of my family's secrets. It wasn't until high school, my grandfather gone for over a decade, that I heard about the accident. The one in the driveway. My grandfather had done it. Hit and killed his own son. Their fifth child. Jerry, they called him.

A Sad Accident

A tragic affair took place on the Art Kottom farm near here Tuesday when Mr. Kottom in moving a truck accidentally hit his young eighteen-month-old son, Gerald. The lad was fatally injured and died while under a doctor's care.

The funeral will be held at the First Lutheran Church of Renville Saturday, at 2 o'clock, Rev. Strom officiating.

The sympathy of the entire community is extended to the stricken family in their hour of sorrow.

—September 26, 1940. *The Renville County Star Farmer*

Because my family has spoken so little of Jerry, I want to unearth his existence. I want to learn about his life, albeit brief. Perhaps this urge tugs harder now that I have children of my own and would not want their histories forgotten. I'm certain if I had learned of Jerry's existence earlier, I could have woven him into my thoughts as I stargazed atop my mother's Pinto in my grandparents' driveway—perhaps in the same spot he was killed. Could have nudged his memory into existence and slowly changed the way things had always been done, in spite of tradition, small towns, and family dynamics. Could have broken the cycle of silence. Perhaps.

(1940) Second summer. An ordinary day. A dusty haze, the stagnant air clenches and recoils against the abnormal heat. Despite the warmth, I imagine my grandmother may have baked Swedish sweet bread early that morning, a family recipe. In *Svenskamerika* Ada had learned the tradition of fika, twice-daily coffee break. From the wood-burning stove, a light breeze delivered outdoors the scent of yeast and cardamom, mingling with manure, sun-drenched hay, and sodden soil, all musty and dank. The eldest daughter had since crossed the gravel road to the one-room schoolhouse, leaving the younger in charge.

Margaret, you've got Jerry, right? my grandmother said, as she brushed the crusty braid with egg white and a sprinkling of sugar. Perhaps Margaret had been distracted, had turned her back, had not heard the backdoor creep open. Hard to hear above a boisterous mother and three spirited brothers. A pale, towheaded toddler roams the yard, chubby legs tottering in a threadbare cloth diaper, safety-pinned and pulled snug. Had Jerry stopped to squat—as children often do to tug at a blade of grass, clasp a dragonfly, puff at a dandelion? Or maybe he had been steering a toy tractor across tire tracks and over anthills.

His father must have been accustomed to checking for children. One last peek in the rearview mirror, one final glance beneath cars, behind bumpers. What had been different this time? Had the boy been in his blind spot? Had shards of sunlight blocked his view? His father may have been distracted—by all the work that lay ahead, all the mouths he had to feed, the looming hours until sundown.

Did he pause, wonder what he'd hit as he backed up the grain truck? Assume it was a tricycle, a raccoon, possibly a farm cat? Or, without a doubt, without a flicker of curious wonder, had his father known upon impact—that slap of a second—what had happened?

Ada, come quick!

Undoubtedly my grandmother raced out the back door to her child. Elbows shoving. *What happened*? Pushing. *Help*. No one to hear. Panicked instructions screeched at Margaret. Bellows of *no, no, no, no*. Orders to get him in the car. *Hurry*. The hospital, an hour away. *Go*.

It all happened so fast.

How does one recover from such loss, such grief and guilt? Did my grandfather lose himself in his thoughts as he sped by the rows of corn, disappear into grave regret? Perhaps he turned to the bottle. Hard to pass judgment, considering all he had been through. When night settled in, blanketing the land in dark despair, had he turned toward those same stars, thrown his hands in the air: *Why has God forsaken me*? Made deals with God, searching for answers, for second chances? For anything? This was avoidable, an accident. There was blame to be placed.

(2008) When I was growing up and my mother was asked how many kids had been in her family, she'd say seven. *Two boys, five girls*. Always the same. Jerry, the brother she never met, the brother who died in the driveway before she was born, was never mentioned. As a teenager, I was confused by his existence: If a sibling died before you are born, did they still count? Did you include them in the tally?

Perhaps my mother weighed her brother's brief existence more heavily as hers was slipping away. She was, after all, the first child born after the accident. His replacement, of sorts.

In the final weeks of her life, her head clouded by cancer, her dignity long since departed, my mother was not herself. The nurses and caretakers asked her questions, sometimes to be polite, sometimes to check what remained of her mind. *How many kids were in your family?* a nurse asked. *Eight*, she said. *Three boys, five girls.* My sister and I exchanged wide-eyed glances. We did not interrogate. I wondered if she felt her brother's presence toward the end, though this was hard to imagine with how little his name had been brought up.

It makes sense that my grandmother crocheted afghans for each of her twenty-one grandchildren when they graduated from high school. As a girl, Ada had been taught the Swedish belief that when troubled it is important to keep one's hands busy. I imagine that at some point after the accident, Ada dug out her Swedish spinning wheel with its twin treadles and large drive wheel, threaded the leader fleece through the loop, and spun: hats, scarves, socks, woolen mittens. If she could not keep her children safe, well, at least she could keep them warm.

(1939) Undoubtedly, like most farm children, Ada's children had been assigned chores. Kenny had been taught how to properly stack the firewood, and the girls to help with the churning, baking, and soap-making. All the kids were assigned to clean the eggs down in the cellar. *Margaret, you've got Jerry, right?* And Jerry—was it Jerry who liked to play with the milk spigot or dip his hands in the cloudy water of the drip bowl? Delores, the eldest daughter, didn't understand why the younger ones had to help with the eggs—they were more of a nuisance, really—but figured her mother appreciated the half hour of peace and quiet to nap or knit. On occasion, Delores would guide her younger siblings' little fingers across the feces- and blood-spattered eggs to include them.

The children made a game of this chore they had grown so tired of. Delores would ask Dick and Jerry the popular Swedish riddle: What is round as an egg and reaches around a church wall? A ball of yarn. Jerry wrinkled up his nose and giggled at the joke, although he could not have possibly understood. Even Margaret, the child who would let her mother down, the child who would never truly forgive herself, joined in on the fun. That, too, was before. Before Margaret had been asked to watch her brother. Before the weight of the world had been shifted onto her knobby, sun-freckled shoulders.

Long before Jerry died, Ada's mother had told her about funerals back home, in the motherland. About how invitations rimmed in black arrived decorously in the post. And how, at home, the bereaved cloaked their windows in ivory sheets, adorned their walkways with finely cut spruce twigs. Services were attended by men dressed in *frack*, white ties and full dress suits; the women, also in black, donned hats with heavy veiling to cover their sorrowful visages. And if the deceased were a parent or spouse, the mourner dressed in black for the entire year, which most likely distressed Ada: the thought of wash day and the endless ironing of black.

Ada must have known Jerry's funeral would be different. The community, however, would still prepare a smorgasbord to be eaten after the services: sandwiches, headcheese, pickled pigs' feet, roast meat, rice pudding. But who could possibly eat at a time like this? Ada had joined the Ladies' Aid Society at church when they first moved to town and, although food preparation had never been her strong suit, was sure to donate pea soup or boiled pork shanks to families in need. What comes around goes around, and all.

(1973) I crawl onto the denim mountain of my grandfather's lap. He's a tall man, sturdy, with enormous hands—rough, calloused palms, dry fingertips, battered fingernails. Sitting on one knee, my sister on the other, my grandfather gently taps and nuzzles the tops of our heads with his cheeks and chin and lips, but with a little pleading, he becomes playful and bounces us. *Like a horse*, we say through our giggles. *Faster*. At two years old, I am not much bigger than Jerry was when he died. And I find it hard to weave my memories of this man, the one whose lap I am perched upon, into what I now imagine of a farmer, a Christian, who once stood beneath the stars, who suffered such loss, who believed the preaching of Ecclesiastes: "To everything there is a season . . . . A time to be born, and a time to die; a time to plant, and a time to pluck up that which is planted." Thirty years earlier he must have rocked his son, too. Although, if he resembles most grandfathers I now know, he did not carve out as much play time for his own children as he did for theirs, especially with all the work that lay ahead, all the mouths he had to feed, the looming hours until sundown.

(1983) It is Sunday morning, and we are at my grandmother's church. My grandmother quickly recognizes people as we walk toward the large wooden doors. *Elsie*, my grandmother bellows above the parking lot din. Indicating my mother, she says, *You remember my daughter LaVaune, the widow*? I speed up, duck inside the arching door frame. I do not want her next words to be about my lack of a father. I do not want her next words to be about me. Would it have been worse if she'd said, LaVaune, the one born after Jerry died? Perhaps Elsie never knew Jerry, but with the way small towns operate, it would not have mattered much.

(1940) My grandmother had always been superstitious—perhaps she clung to anxieties passed down from her parents. Before the first full moon of the new year, toting a sack of meat or bread in one hand and a hymnbook in the other, her father may have stood sternly before the moonlit sky—for he believed his fate to be written in the stars. While Ada pointed out the Little Dipper, her *pappa* would glide his fingers across the scriptures of a brushed-open Bible page. He believed, like many farmers before him, that the words he read, and the deciphered messages, would determine the fate of the upcoming farming season. Not Ada. Not my practical grandmother. She would have thought any verse could be rephrased to her family's advantage, which she suspected her father of doing from time to time. Her mother, equally superstitious, had also adopted the anxieties of her ancestors and shivered over the possibility of thirteen diners at any given table. She also fretted over black cats—bad things were bound to happen if a black cat crossed in front of your automobile. But this was all before. When superstitions were just that. Nothing, really. Did Ada ever wonder, just once—for a brief moment—if there was something she could have done, some superstition she could have abided by to prevent the death of her son, of Baby Jerry?

Ada recalled how her mother worried whenever she and her sister frolicked near the stream behind the barn. To keep them safe, she told the girls about Näcken, the water sprite who would tug you under and never release you if you were not careful. Ada recalled the admonishments of her mother, spoken in a

Swedish accent so strong that it ironed out the j sound, and "angel" became "an-yel." *My an-yels, do not forget Näcken. He's lonely and loves the company of small children.* Did Ada ever wonder if there was a sprite who tugged small children beneath truck tires, never to let go? The sprites, the black cats, one's fate written in the stars—deep down she knew it was all *sopa.* Rubbish.

After Ada's grandmother passed, Ada's mother, in accordance with Swedish custom, displayed a photograph of her late mother on the mantel, alongside a small mason jar. Each day, following tradition, Ada's mother made sure the makeshift vase held a fresh tulip or daisy for an entire year. Did Ada do this for Jerry? Most likely not, since they didn't own many photographs —only a couple were shot of the boy after his birth and one at his christening. Plus, everyone knew Ada was not much of a gardener.

Weeks after Jerry's funeral, when fewer people came to visit, Ada recalled a Swedish nursery rhyme she had heard her mother recite to her at bedtime or when either she or her sister scraped an elbow or knee. Ada could sing the Swedish lyrics but needed her mother to translate:

Hush hush, child.
The cat is tangled in the yarn.
Hush hush child
The cat is tangled in mother's yarn.

Perhaps Ada thought of the bedtime story she'd read to the boys—Richard and Kenny and Baby Jerry—mere days before the accident. *Snippy and Snappy* is a sweet tale about two field mice who, while playing with their mother's ball of yarn, wander away from home and end up in a nearby farmhouse. Just as Snappy is about to nibble at the cheese in a mousetrap, his father jumps in to rescue him, to return him safely home.

Yarn. Was it yarn that passed through Ada's mind as she settled in for a night of knitting? How it all goes back to Mother's yarn?

I like to imagine, long before the bad things happened, all the good in the lives of my grandparents. In the early years of their marriage, shortly after Ada and Art had built the farmhouse, Art planted fruit and shade trees around the property. Ada recalled one spring, how the two of them linked arms and, through the second-floor windows, gazed proudly upon their property—the blossoming apple trees, the freshly painted crimson barn, the endless rows of wheat. Ada remembered how dry the previous summer had been, how the brittle corn leaves rustled like newspaper when the hot wind blew, and how they used to worry so about the crops, about the future. But on this day, an afternoon so unlike any of a second summer, Ada could not deny her happiness.

(1993) We are back in Renville for my grandmother's funeral. Although gone, she lingers in her home. The scent of Vaseline lotion, Starlight mints, and tight, stale air crowd the room—all forlorn remnants of a life that has passed. During the day, we imagine her sitting at the kitchen table, her brittle hair wound around puffy rollers, scribbling away at the pages of puzzle books. Evenings are different. No more Bible verses recited at a deafening pitch. From the book of James, she'd choose verses with a personal slant: "Therefore be patient, brethren, until the coming of the Lord. The farmer waits for the precious produce of the soil, being patient about it, until it gets the early and late rains." On those nights, in the next room, my cousins and I would cup our fingers to stifle our giggles, although she couldn't possibly have heard us with her increasing deafness and the drone of her own voice. As she read Scripture, did she think of Jerry, the child who lived but eighteen months? Remind herself that God only dishes out as much as you can handle? Recall the good-intentioned phrases heard decades earlier: *He's in a better place, or he's God's newest angel.* And though she was a Christian woman, a God-fearing one at that, did she know this too was *sopa*?

We arrive at the church for the funeral service. My cousins and I shuffle into a chipped wooden pew near the front—the last time we had been together in this church was for my uncle's funeral, seven years earlier, and once before that at my grandfather's funeral, when I was four, though it is disputed whether or not I actually attended the service. On this day, the day we lay our grandmother to rest, my sister reaches into the wooden pocket before her and pulls out a tattered hymnbook. Inside the front cover, it reads, "In loving memory of Gerald Kottom, 1940." I feel a stab of discomfort—a pale shade of budding guilt?—because we had not thought of the boy, of Jerry, not even at the funeral of his mother. If he was not to be remembered on this day, then when?

Silence—that I know. After my dad died when I was nine, we did not talk about him. I learned not to ask questions or bring up memories, as my mother's eyes would turn glassy, her nostrils moist and red, her downturned lips quivery—a silent prelude to her weeping. My mother had not been taught to deal with death, to speak of grief. When nothing is said of the sibling who died before you were born, how do you learn? Perhaps family secrets become tangled when home is a place you are straddling, with one foot on the soil of your birthplace and another stretched an ocean away. I wonder how many years passed before my mother heard the details of the accident, and I wonder how the facts had been parceled out. All in one big heap? Or perhaps she had been cast threads of information each second summer, just as the heat stood still, as her parents could not help but think of Jerry. Her mother may have shown her a photograph of him, let her smooth the ragged fur of his stuffed bear, sniff his beloved blanket, but did she ever hear about the stars and the knitting and the sprites and the stifling heat?

My grandmother would not approve of what I've written—secrets spilled about a child spoken so little about. But I like to imagine things differently for their family, because the silence surrounding my father hurt. I now talk about my mother's death with my sons, who were six and two when she died.

I am not silent.

When My Mother Ironed,
It Felt Choreographed

If it were a dance, it would be a waltz. *Step step close*. Set to a silent ballad, I could feel the glide in her rhythm, as if she'd been driven by an inner aria. Her iron, guiding her like a bow across a bass viol—tender, with wild control. I'd crouch next to the bookcase and hum, swaying along in my desire to belong.

A duet of sorts. Me and her, back and forth and back. Happy we were—months before Dad's heart gave way, before cancer drove holes through her brain, which felt like tunnels. *Step step close*.

How to Activate Your AncestryDNA Kit

Do NOT eat, drink, smoke, or chew gum for thirty minutes before giving your saliva sample.

Do NOT expect to find you have a half-brother. When you find out he'd been born nine years before you and had been placed up for adoption, drink, smoke, eat—do whatever you need to do.

Fill the tube with saliva to the black wavy line.

Fill in your aunts and uncles, ask if they knew your dad was aware he had a son. Find out he didn't. Tell your half-brother that his biological father died of a heart attack when you were nine. Ask your half-brother about his cholesterol. Disguise your jealousy when he says he is the picture of health.

Fill the tube until your saliva is at or just above the wavy line. It's easy—that's less than ¼ teaspoon. Do not overfill.

Fill in your half-brother about yourself and sister, or plan to. It's easy—there won't be much to say because he won't ask many questions. Be prepared to listen to lots of bragging. Don't act surprised when he says he's the smartest guy in any room. Overfill? Oh, he will.

Replace the funnel with the cap.

Replace what you think he'd ask about your father. Refrain from telling him that a nine-year-old does not think of her father in that way when his only question is if your father was smart.

Despite your wishes, he won't ask if your dad had a good sense of humor, if he played Barbies with you, or took you boating at your cabin up North. He won't ask if he let you style his hair, roll strands into pink styrofoam curlers, or use rubber bands to clump his black locks into short stumps. Won't ask if he took you and your sister out for rum and butter sundaes when your mom worked nights.

Was he a good dad? Nope, he won't ask that either.

Remove the funnel from the tube. Screw on the enclosed cap tightly to release the solution that will stabilize the DNA in your saliva.

Remove any expectations you have, anything to stabilize your emotions.

Tighten to release stabilizing fluid.

Tighten your seatbelts. Despite the red flags, you will plan a trip to meet him in his hometown.

You will know it works when the blue solution from the cap has emptied into the tube.

You'll know it's not working when he tells you he is upset that you won't meet him at his house, but at this point you are no more than strangers. You will know it's not working when he wants to cancel the trip three days before you are to leave.

Keep DNA kit out of reach of children.

Keep half-brother out of reach of your children.

Warning: Do not ingest the stabilizing solution in the tube cap.

Warning: Do not ingest your doubts. Go. Allow him into your life, meet his wife and children. He is, after all, a link to your father, and there are not many left. Like him, your sons are adopted and you can only hope their biological siblings would be as receptive.

If your skin, eyes, or mouth come in contact with the solution, wash with water.

If his skin, eyes, or mouth resemble your father's, don't be startled. His voice, too. This commonality will mess with your head, and it'll feel like you've been given a chance to know your father as an adult.

Shake the tube for at least five seconds.

Shake (and cry) for five seconds. Five minutes. Five hours. Two months after you have met, he will tell you he no longer wants you in his life. By then, you will have created a bond with his daughters—your only nieces from your side of the family. He looks like your father, and it will feel like you are losing him all over again.

This will ensure your sample mixes thoroughly with the stabilizing solution, so our lab can best process your sample.

> This will ensure that you are no longer stable. A lab? Try a therapist's office. You will need to schedule emergency sessions.

Place the tube in the collection bag.

> Place a simple text: "Best of luck to you and your family." Be prepared for him to change his mind and message you three weeks later stating he wants you back.

Place the sample inside the collection bag provided in your DNA kit. Seal the bag with an adhesive strip.

> Place a text to your half-brother. Remind him you'd warned him about your abandonment issues and your fear that he'd disregarded those feelings. (Not once, but twice.) Once again, wish his family the best of luck.

Mail in your sample.

> Do not mail him again.

~~When your results are ready, we'll contact you at the email address associated with your Ancestry account. After that, you'll be able to access your personalized results anytime at Ancestry.com.~~

Disregard; you'll never be ready.

Greeting Cards

I didn't attend school the week of my dad's funeral. When I returned, the thaw had not yet come. Mounds of snow lined the streets and sidewalks. Ice soaked through my mittened hands as I glided them over the snowbanks.

Jimmy, one of five hearing-impaired students, stopped me in the cloak room. *Sorry your dad died*, he signed. *Thank you*, I signed back. No one else looked me in the eye. When I opened my desk, I didn't see any sympathy cards, like the ones we made out of construction paper for each other's birthdays. Beneath my desk, I rolled over my flattened hands, signed: *Dead.* Is he dead? I bent my wrist, moved my fist up and down. *Yes*, I signed. *He is dead.*

Snowball

You press your palms into the painted cinder blocks, glide your fingers along the grooved cracks. Dig the toe break of one skate into the slick floor—stationing, grounding yourself, telling yourself that you belong. That you belong here as much as the next girl. You roll the wheels of the other skate back and forth, almost imperceptibly, as if it feels normal, commonplace even, to stand here alongside this wall, waiting.

You do not mention, not to anyone, that you spent an entire day's worth of your mother's wages on your outfit. She is single, and there is only one paycheck. You hope what you're wearing today will increase your odds of getting noticed. With the dimmed lights and twinkle of the disco ball, your shirt glows in the dark.

Earlier in the week your mother took you shopping, bought you this white woven top and a pair of designer jeans. You do not usually shop at the mall. The mall is reserved for other girls: the ones waiting further down the wall. Those girls, whose bodies are sculpted by ballet and gymnastics. Girls who show off their trim bodies in snug-fitting jeans, confident they'll be approached by the cute boys who can skate backward. Those girls, when they attempt to color their own hair and screw up, have mothers who allow them to skip school, take them to the fancy salon downtown to get it fixed. You? You are stuck with uneven streaks of mustard and platinum until it grows out.

Before your mother dropped you off at the rink, you spent an hour feathering your hair, parting it down the middle, spraying it still with White Rain, even though White Rain makes you sneeze. Your bangs will fall flat without it, and your chances of being asked to skate are already slim.

As the lights dim and the music softens, those other girls, the ones who hum along to the music and giggle amongst themselves, they know they will not wait long. Those girls date high school boys. Those girls have mothers who tuck extra quarters into their backpacks so they can buy Dr Pepper and Jolly Ranchers from the corner store after school.

When the last few boys skate by and you realize they are not headed your way, you crouch down to re-lace your skate, twirl the ends of your hair. When all of the single skaters are paired up—even the neighbor boy who gave you a Valentine's Day gift in the fifth grade—you rush off to the bathroom, over to the concession stand. Act relieved to avoid the crowds.

You glance down at your hands and realize the blue of your denim has bled onto your fingers, onto the frayed edges of your new top. You wish you had not clipped the sales tags so you could return them both. It'll take you decades to forgive yourself for spending $68 on this outfit. To realize your mother had worked eight hours at the hospital for a pair of jeans and one shirt. Eight hours, and you were not asked to skate for a single minute.

Evening Out the Sides

There was a time when my children were orphans. There was a time before I became one. My younger son and I were never orphans at the same time; we missed an overlap by seven months. He was gaining parents while I was losing mine. When I adopted Jack months before my mother died, I had been balancing the number of parents in the world. That need for balance—I know it well. I felt it as a child; it manifested as Obsessive Compulsive Disorder, or OCD. When I was nine, I lost my father, and as if to balance that loss, my limbs compensated with too much movement, too much awareness, too much repetition—anything to take my mind off of my worry.

To calm my nerves, I counted.

1. When I was a child, I had to make sure my right and left sides experienced touch the same. If my right arm swiped a door frame, I'd need to step back into the doorway to swipe my left arm. If I stepped on three sidewalk cracks with my left foot, I'd do the same with my right. Left, Left, Left. Right, Right, Right. The degree and duration of each touch mattered. Did I need to recreate a stomp or a fairy-light tiptoe? Had it been a drawn-out dusting of my left shoulder or a clap-length press? In my mind, I was "evening out the sides." If I didn't, something bad might happen.

My grandmother gave me a 5x7 cardboard picture of Jesus. It was bright orange and yellow and sat on my nightstand. I kissed that photo three times in the morning, three times after school, and three times at night. Kissed it to the point that some of the cardboard wore off and parts of his face were missing.

In the third grade I concluded any paragraph written for school with "Period," "The End," and an actual punctuation mark of a period. My teacher, Ms. Weitrich, would cross the words out and write, "Just one single period." When I refused to stop writing my three-part finale, she gave up. Once, toward the end of the school year, she stuck a smiley face sticker next to the series of endings and wrote, "Amen."

It was weeks after my father died from a heart attack that my symptoms first appeared. Genetics play a role in the development of OCD, but stress is also a factor. My mother never reported any of my unusual behavior to a doctor, so I never sought help. And, like most things in my family, we never talked about it. Amen. Amen. AMEN.

***

When I became an orphan, within months of my son's adoption, it seemed the universe had been doing the same as me—restoring balance. When my mother was sick and her death imminent, I saw myself as an ORPHAN. The word was unavoidable, accusatory. The word itself was blaring. Odd, though, because I'd never used "orphan" to describe my own children; I referred to that period of their lives as "when they lived in Russia" or "before they came home." Rather than say they lived in an orphanage, I prefered the Russian term of Baby Home, any title that included *home*. Home, home, HOME.

2. I took my spot nearest the nightstand, my mother kneeled next to me, and my sister settled in on her other side. I waited until they both matched my positioning, until all three of us were kneeling up high against my bed, our hands folded prayer style—fingers crossed, not pressed together—with our elbows propped up on my Holly Hobbie bedspread.

I began. "Our father with Art in heaven—" My grandpa's name was Art and that was how I thought it was said.

At the end, in unison, we said, "Amen." I then repeated, "Amen," a little louder, all by myself.

I led into the next, "Hail Mary full of Grace." By now my family knew the routine; the same three prayers were to be recited in the same order.

We were nearing the prayer's end: "now and at—ACHOO—the hour of our death." I stopped; I needed to know who had sneezed.

My mother turned to me, urging me along with her widened eyes. In the past, when anyone would cough or yawn or flub a word, we needed to start over from the beginning, start again with the Our Father. I understood my mother's frustration at this moment; it was getting late and we had almost finished two of the three prayers. But, no, I knew it'd been Beth's mouse-sized sneeze; she'd been the one to make me lose focus.

"That's it." I shot my sister a dirty look. "From the top." (Again, Again, AGAIN.) I bowed my head and closed my eyes. "Our father with Art—'"

Toward the end of the Glory Be, during, "As it was in the beginning is now," I smelled the salty, buttery aroma of freshly made popcorn, and knew Beth, who selected a spot nearest the door, had escaped. My mother had stayed. Going forward, it would be my sister I could count on more, the one who would stay. The one who would count.

***

Meeting new people, social situations where he doesn't feel in control, starting new things—my younger son Jack has had his own share of anxiety. He has been diagnosed with ADHD and dyslexia; most children who share either diagnosis also experience anxiety. In the first grade, he developed a tic: an incessant clearing of his throat. It continued for years and was most noticeable before any stressful event, like the beginning of each school year. He now attends a private school for those with dyslexia and ADHD, and his tics have almost disappeared. Occasionally, I hear an extra clearing of his throat—two, sometimes three in a row—but no one else in my family notices, and I wonder if I am imagining it. I never point it out, not to anyone; it seems to be a language he only uses with me. A language only detected by the anxious.

3. Each day during middle school, as we waited for her to return from work, my sister and I would hang out in our mother's bedroom. She had the biggest bed, the most delicate bottles, the most ornate-looking lipsticks. The room and her drawer contents—the neatly folded silken slips, the lace and satin nighties—smelled like her cologne, as she called it, musky and warm. Our video games were set up in there, and on my turn, my sister would sprawl out on Mom's down comforter, her homework fanned out before her. I'd scoot to the bed's edge, my face inches from the television set.

One afternoon, on level three of *Ms. Pac-Man* glanced into the mirror behind the dresser. I stopped. The left side of my face had frozen. It was no longer matching the right. When I smiled, only the right side of my face curled into a grin. When I lifted my brow, only the right side arched.

I reached behind and tapped my sister on the leg. She toppled over her spelling book and folders as she moved toward the dresser. "Watch this." I smiled. We both studied my reflection's half grin.

She shook her head as if to say, "So what?"

I flared out my right nostril, in and out, in and out. "Weird," she said. "Now make a mad face." Two different emotions emerged—the right side scowled while the left side stood still.

Beth orchestrated my next expressions. "Do a surprised face, now a scared one. Try sad." Sad, happy, sad, happy, SAD.

We rarely called our mother at the hospital where she worked as a nurse because we knew how busy she was. This, however, felt important. While I studied my face, Beth ran to the kitchen, to the house phone mounted on the wall.

As my sister made her way back into the bedroom, I caught her reflection in the mirror, her flattened smile. "Mom sounds worried. She's coming home." I turned from the mirror, no longer finding my face as humorous. It was rare for my mom to leave work early—the only other time had been five years before, the time I'd fallen off of the bathroom counter and needed emergency surgery. This time I was afraid I might get into trouble, as if I could have prevented my uneven expressions like I should have prevented my clumsy dismount from the sink that had led to stitches.

When my mother got home, she rushed around, ordering me into the car. "Go. Go. Go." I slid across the vinyl back seat, tried to catch my reflection in her rearview mirror, wondering if any of my neighbors had been watching the commotion and noticed something was off. If it were a true emergency—it did feel that way—maybe my mother should have called an ambulance. Perhaps she thought she'd be faster in her olive-green Pinto as she sped to the hospital, to the children's ER next door to where she'd just left.

The doctors performed a few quick tests, diagnosed my unevenness as Bell's palsy, and prescribed prednisone. I liked the attention from the pretty nurses, some of whom were my mom's friends from the hospital next door. I kept hearing: "How is she? Do you need me to do anything?"

Once the medicine had kicked in, my mother revealed she'd been worried I'd had a stroke. For her, Bell's palsy was a relief. I recovered within weeks and didn't need physical therapy or any further treatment. I'd never had physical therapy—perhaps my mother didn't believe in therapy of any kind—and wondered if I would have gotten a lot of attention like I did at the hospital. Either way, my sides were evened out. I was fortunate since some people with Bell's palsy never regain use of half of their face. My mother spoke of a doctor she worked with whose mouth sagged his entire life, possible proof for her of therapy's ineffectiveness. For him, there'd been no shot at balance.

***

While I was counting cracks in the sidewalk, grabbing door knobs, citing and reciting prayers, a childhood friend who'd lost her brother had developed a disorder similar. In junior high, my friend twirled clumps of glossy black hair between her thumb and forefinger, and once it was tightly wound, she'd scratch her handful of hair. Taut like a rubber band, the sound would reverberate throughout the classroom. This friend was tiny—no one expected such a sound to come from her. I never found either her or her behavior to be strange. Instead, I was more curious, and relieved that I wasn't the only oddball.

4. My sister claims my unusual OCD-type behavior began when I was younger, before our dad died. She recalls the time our mother took us to have breakfast with Santa at Dayton's, the fancy department store downtown. Mrs. Claus, Santa, and the elves would sing Christmas carols while we ate our silver dollar pancakes and

greasy sausage links. Afterward, everyone would line up to get their photos taken with the cast. During "Jingle Bells," as I was trying to clap along to its beat of three, Jing-le-Bells, Jing-le-Bells, I panicked. I couldn't hear. The other kids were banging their forks against their plates, pounding their fists into the table, and shrieking out the lyrics. My mother beckoned an elf over to our group, anything to get me to stop crying. The elf, in her striped stockings and pointy ears, kneeled down beside my chair, and just to me, sang "Jingle Bells."

By high school, my OCD had gone away, though it resurfaces when I'm overwhelmed. I was taking graduate classes and waiting tables at night when I first began teaching. On occasion, I would leave my house and need to return home to make sure that I'd turned off the coffee pot, the iron, lock the door, anything. Once, I needed to leave school in the middle of class because I was convinced my negligence was going to burn my apartment down. After that, each morning, I'd allow an extra ten minutes or so to check and recheck appliances and locks. Off, on, off, on, OFF.

***

My children do not seem to mind when others find out they are adopted. There is no shame. No secrecy. At their ages, I was too embarrassed to admit I didn't have a father—I didn't want to be seen as different. When someone asked me what my parents did for a living, I'd avoid the question, or lie. Once when friends were over, weeks after my father had passed, a telemarketer called the house and asked to speak to my father. My mother had taken the call and all we heard was, "He's dead." She was telling the truth, and there was nothing wrong with her reply, but I was ashamed that my friends had to hear that, had been subjected to my family's secrets, had been privy to our sorrow. We all know he's dead, I wanted to scream. Dead. Dead. DEAD.

***

Months before my dad died, I tried to imagine what life would have been like if my father weren't around. Back then, I never allowed myself to wonder the same about my mother—that would've been disastrous and unbearable. I never told anyone that I felt responsible for his death and held onto this guilt throughout my childhood. He was alive one minute, dead the next. (Undead, dead, undead, dead. DEAD.) My sister blamed herself, too. Beth had been dealing with neighborhood bullies and desperately wanted a friend. She'd made a bargain with God—she was willing to sacrifice our father in exchange for one loyal friend, just one. (One, none, one, none, ONE.) I still will not allow myself to imagine the worst of life's scenarios, as if my thoughts might provide the universe with an idea that it finds too tantalizing, too alluring to ignore.

5. Seven years ago, my anxiety and depression reached an all time high. I worried about everything, and it affected my self-esteem. Depression is powerful. When you are in the dredges, you do not see things clearly—at that point, it can be nearly impossible to pull yourself out. I'd do what one of my therapists had suggested; in a series of three, I'd repeat: "You have a family who loves you. You have a family who loves you unconditionally. You have a family who loves you, and you are lucky for that." As I'd witnessed in group therapy, not everyone can say that about their own families.

Several Novembers ago, in a moment of great sadness and desperation, I asked my husband why he even loved me. He rattled off a few things, but also wrote a more thorough list and emailed it to me. He said he didn't want me to ever be left wondering.

***

There is a peculiar guilt among adoptive mothers—guilt over the length of time our children spent without us, whether it be in an orphanage or with a foster family. If only we had found our child sooner. If only we hadn't delayed our decision to adopt. If only we had completed the loads of paperwork quicker. A friend who'd gone through fertility treatments blamed herself for not ditching the pregnancy route sooner, certain those futile months of needles and thermometers could have been better spent searching for her Chinese son.

I imagine the checking and rechecking of temperatures and tests, the counting and recounting of days and shots, the imbalance in one's hormones and bodies. And the guilt from not getting any of that right either. Not pregnant. Pregnant? NOT PREGNANT.

6. I can still imagine my mother's hugs—light, high on my upper back, her palms flat, her elbows tilted upward. A soft pat, pat, pat. The last time she embraced me, weeks before she died, it was too quick, too soft, and I can no longer feel

it. No impression had been left on my back. If only it had been tighter, more indelible. Something to balance out the longing I have for more time with her; something to fill in for the time I wish I'd had with my sons. Pat, pat, PAT.

We had been waiting months for a court date to finalize our older son's adoption, and had traveled to Russia to visit him. At the end of our stay, we were forced to leave him behind, not knowing how long it would be until we saw him again.

We always said our farewells in the play area, the room down the hall from the one where he slept—fifteen cots lined up soldier-style, in rows of three, head to footboard. With sheets tucked tightly into the mattresses, the fluffed pillows looked like little birds ready to bounce into flight. In the play area, a ruby-red carpet covered the wooden floors. Spices from the day's lunch of borscht and perogies had made their way into the bedroom, tempting the children's hunger for more food, more love. More. A reminder that this place would always leave them wanting.

I had learned some Russian and, on our second trip, as we were saying goodbye, I whispered, "Ya tibia Lyblu." I love you.

He stared at me, and with his sweet raspy voice, said, "Lyblu?" Love you? A question.

Tight, with hands that seemed too big for a two-year-old, he reached around my waist and squeezed. He then turned, shot off to join his group at the Baby Home, as if he'd be seeing us the next day and the next, unaware the wait would be months. I watched my son run off wearing almost nothing, in an undershirt, tights, and his little red sandals. Watched him dart past the potted plants and fogged-up windows, watched until he turned the corner and was out of sight.

On the thirteen-hour flight home, from Moscow to Minneapolis, I'd replay what he'd said and imagine his clenched arms, his little boy smell of sweat and wind, his inability to comprehend love. I liked to imagine that months later when he hugged the giant Teddy bear in the common area, he conjured me: my skinny arms, my freckled hands. The desperation in my embrace.

Period. The End. .

Taming Your Prognosis

I wasn't crying because the bleach I'd used to clean your dishrags ruined my sweatshirt. I was crying because you only had a few months to live. Because I was thirty-six and had already lost one parent. Crying because I knew your brain would slowly give out and the doctor said surgery, our only hope, would make you worse. When I sat on the couch next to you, you set down the *TV Guide*. I tucked my head into your collarbone—you pulled me closer. Cried more when you promised to buy me a new sweatshirt. Pressed against your chest, I said I was going to miss you, that I wished I could s l o w   d o w n   time. Tame your prognosis, I would have said, though I didn't allow beautiful words around those feelings. Not yet. A decade before I saw beauty in this moment.

Mom's Cigarettes

After Dad left for work, Mom, with her coffee and ashtray within reach, would settle into a seat at the kitchen table and phone her girl-friends. Kathy and Barb and Jody from Brain-erd. "Hang on," she'd say while she pulled in her cheeks, inhaled what looked like freedom. I'd listen from the hallway as she sputtered out laughter, a cough here and there. Watch as she stubbed out the tiniest nub of a cigarette, her pencil-thin fingers twisting and grinding.

One night when Mom was at work, Dad asked if we had a lighter. I told him that Mom must have one since she smoked. He shook his head, said nothing. Later that night I woke to Dad yelling. I poked my head out of my bed-room door and watched him shoving my mother up against the wall, his calloused hands wrapped around her slim neck. Instead of saying anything, I tucked back into the safety of my bedroom, knowing that her fear was my fault. The next day I offered a quiet apology. "Oh punky, you didn't do anything wrong," she said and kissed the top of my head.

A few years later when I was nine, my dad died. Just days after his funeral, Mom pulled into the lot of the nearby convenience store. "Why don't you two go grab a treat?" My sister grabbed an Almond Joy, and I picked out Reese's Pieces. At the checkout counter, my mom asked for a pack of Camel Lights—I hadn't seen her smoke since that night with Dad, but I figured she did since the phone receiver still smelled like her bitter, smoker's breath.

I never did witness her smoke that pack of cigarettes. Maybe she lit up outside on the back steps, maybe it was on the nights she stayed up late talking to her sisters, as she twisted the phone cord around her tucked-up knees—her smokey laughter replaced by whispers and worry. I wonder if on those nights her cigarettes tasted like anything but freedom.

Cleaning Up His Messes

Discarded socks and belts. Magazine leaflets, ripped and tossed. Gnawed-on Styrofoam coffee cups. My father left messes wherever he went. At the dinner table, he managed to create the most crumbs; even his water glasses left the thickest rings. As he plowed from the TV room to the bathroom or kitchen, my mother would trail behind—reaching and wiping, tucking trash beneath her armpits, chinning clothes against her chest.

On this morning, the sun shone brightly, streaming like bullets through the front windows. My mother tidied up the kitchen while my older sister Beth and I lounged on the living room floor. My father, wearing boxer shorts and a white T-shirt with pits that hadn't yet yellowed, had spread out on a nearby couch. His hairy fingers leafed through the sports pages while the rest of the Sunday paper lay scattered—an open page dangled from the coffee table, comics butted up against his thick runner's thigh, and a glossy Colgate ad stuck to his big toe.

Beth and I were busy filling in color-by-number books, shading in the orange spaces with amber, rust, and butterscotch. My father called our names. We stopped. He was never the first to talk to us; we knew this must be important. As I slid crayons back into the box, my father folded and pressed the pages together as best he could, the usual extent of his cleaning.

We crawled over, Beth and I, and knelt in front of his dry, flaky feet. Athlete's foot, I was to later learn. His breath smelled like old grape juice, bitter and moldy. Beth gathered stray sheets of newspaper until my father raised his hand, motioning her to stop.

He ran his fingers through his thick, black curls. *I need to tell you something about Grandma T.,* he said. Grandma's shiny dentures, softly cool cheeks, and girlish giggle came to mind. In the next room, my mother slammed drawers, clanked dishes. *Quiet it down,* he shouted. Looking away, he told us Grandma T. was not his real mother, that there had been someone before her. Beth's eyebrows arched into crescent moons above her dark, hollow eyes.

***

It is unclear why he chose this particular time to share such news. Had the way we'd been calmly quiet while our mother fidgeted in the kitchen and he read the paper reminded him of his childhood? Perhaps he had known that tableau well, felt secure enough in the stability of our Sunday morning routine to tell us right then. Done correctly and with my mother's approval, this conversation could have served as a primer on death, a discussion we would be needing to have soon.

As we sat before him, he told us his real mom had died when he was six, my age at the time. My mother briefly flicked on the garbage disposal. *She'd been sick for a year*, he continued. The kitchen noises stopped. *I always thought she was going to get better, even when she could barely get out of bed*. Reminded of the time my mom had been sick with the flu, I began to wail. Near-silent staccato gasps escaped from Beth's mouth, her heaving shoulders finally giving way to tears. *Could use a little help in here*, was the way my father chose to exit the conversation, eventually exit the room. He'd always preferred an exit over an entrance.

My mother had already been closing in, although he hadn't noticed. Her eyes narrowed at my father sitting on the couch, at her two

71

daughters limp on a blanket of crumpled newspapers, the pages now moist from tears and sweat. I tucked myself into a ball, covered my ears. Flexible and skinny, my sister hugged her limbs. Within seconds my mother had gathered us both, shuffled us over to our chair—the velvet one with the soft, golden arms—to shelter us from our father's anger. He had not considered the toll of his hurried news. We had ruined his peaceful morning.

The three of us sat entwined. After some moments passed, my mother's need to comfort us waned, replaced by her need to tidy up. Dad would be gone, dead from a heart attack within three years. No amount of straightening could have prepared her for that. But for now, my mother looked at her daughters, at her husband's mess of papers, and knew it was time to pick up. A light, feather dusting, really; the heavy lifting was yet to come.

Signs

On the way up North, I spot a sign on the side of the road: ADOPT-A-HIGHWAY. Girl Scout Troop #273 had claimed this one, must have donated money from their cookie sales and worn orange neon vests as they clutched and stabbed garbage that had gripped the road's edges. Greasy hamburger wrappers, cigarette butts, sun-bleached aluminum cans, yesterday's news. Those shoulders, a haven for sobriety tests and radar guns. Hitchhikers and roadkill. Trash.

*

Six months after I got engaged—and not quite ready to consider children—I wanted a kitten. At the Humane Society, I scanned the walls of homeless pets. Soul after unwanted soul. The screeches and scratching, clanging of cages and keys, yelps from the back, the sorrowful stench of urine. I passed an older cat—those deep-set eyes, that emptiness—its owners had moved out of the country, or so it read on the sign. A brown tabby rubbed her fur up against the metal wires, purred when I squeezed my fingers in to scratch behind her ears. As if fate had brought us together, I brought her home that night, an eight-year-old named Peanut. Needing her to know she was wanted, that she was mine, I whispered, "I would never leave the country without you."

*

When I'd proven to myself that I could be nurturing, it was time for a baby. Our route? International adoption, even though we knew the journey could be long and painful. We wanted a girl, an infant preferably.

DETOUR

I was browsing photos on a website that featured orphans older than two. It seemed like an unusual way to learn about available children, but nothing of our adoption journey had seemed ordinary—not the three sets of fingerprints, the multiple home visits, the extensive background checks, the letters of reference. This website referred to them as "Waiting Children." First names only, a brief description. No country of origin. I was drawn to one boy's somber face, his almond-shaped eyes, his furrowed brow, how he'd been described as "serious and stoic." We eventually brought him home from Siberia: a giggling three-year-old named Grisha.

*

It costs $200-$600 a month to adopt a highway, a fraction of what it costs to rent a billboard. The website uses "sponsor" interchangeably with "adopt." No political candidates or slogans. No "In Memory of" or slander. Two clean-ups required a year—a bargain for all of that advertising. All of that goodwill.

*

Because it took a year to bring our son home, we traveled to Russia four times. Even though he was two when we met him, the orphanage caretaker insisted he was potty-trained. It didn't always seem that way, so we bought him disposable diapers to wear. In between visits—and once he was settled back at the orphanage—

the employees said he'd wrap himself in any given rag, tuck and fold the sides around his tiny waist and squeeze.

*

The hairstylist misted my hair, combed it straight. "So what does he call you?" I must have looked confused. "That little boy, the one you adopted." *My son, you mean*? Too shaken to say anything. Wished I'd been quick enough to ask what she called her mother, though there'd been many signs that it wouldn't have made a difference.

*

There is a common misconception that people adopt because they are altruistic. Some say my adopted children are lucky. None of this is true, not with my family. My husband and I needed our children as much as they needed us. No altruism here. Goodwill better find a different place to call home.

*

Our home is not clean carpets and floors, not pets shooed off tables and countertops. It is not proper language and manners, nor strict schedules and rules. It is a place to feel loved. It is a place where my husband and I apologize to our kids when we say the wrong things, apologize to each other. It is a place where we celebrate that our kids are adopted—pets, too—but we do not dwell on it. It is a place where every being who lives here has been chosen, a place where everyone belongs.

*

I don't want my children to ever feel disheartened by the term "adopt," as if adopting a highway and a pet and a child are equal. Words are just words, I tell them, and aren't always appropriate. Should there be a new term, I ask my younger son, who is now fourteen. To get him thinking, I suggest, "embrace" or "chosen." He says, "Brought-in child," as if he'd been waiting his entire life for this question.

Citizen

Have you heard about the boy whose parents shipped him back to Russia, by himself, with just a note? The adoption wasn't working, or so they'd written on a letter that they'd pinned to his chest.

I bet stories like this scare you, but I want you to know not one of these stories is about your son. My son now. Mine. Whenever a similar story hits the news, I think of you. I am sure you wonder what happened to the child you kept for eight months—over 200 days to love, to feed, to bathe, to read to at bedtime—the boy you cared for enough to place for adoption.

Do you ever wonder where he lives now? If he has siblings? How I found him? Because he was older, he was placed on an international waiting list. I saw a photograph, his birthday, his first name. There was something about his sweet, somber face that made me feel he belonged to me, as I like to believe you once thought, too. A black and white photograph, that was all I had. I didn't know where he lived, only that I was drawn to an imagined personality, all gleaned from a single image.

On one of my four trips to Russia—they weren't going to give him to just anyone—I begged to meet you. I wanted his medical history. I wanted to look for a resemblance. I wanted to tell you in person what I am telling you now—that he would be cared for. The head orphanage doctor knew you, but refused to arrange a meeting, saying, "It never ends well. There will always be jealousy." I didn't understand. I still don't. It seemed he wanted to protect you, protect me, protect his country. Or perhaps, he was simply doing his job.

Do you know I received videos of him, ones taken from when he was first sent to live in the orphanage and then more recent ones? As time passed and as the footage showed, he went from being lively and cheerful to somber and earnest. This tells me he had once been happy, happy to be with you, happy to have you as his mother.

Although I have many questions, there are so many things you have done right. According to the hospital's records, my son was born healthy—and he continues to thrive—so I know that during your pregnancy you took care of yourself. In the first video I saw of him, taken after the time he had lived with you, he looked robust. When I speak of his infancy—to him or to anyone who asks—this is what I focus on.

Because you knew the head doctor, did you ever ask about your baby? I am sure you must have been curious. When you gave up your rights, you were not allowed to visit—time spent with your child would disrupt any probability of him ever being adopted—and, according to court records, you never did, which must have been unbearable, especially since you lived in the same city.

He is mine now, but he will always be a citizen of both our countries—a citizen of you, a citizen of me. Someday, he could return to Russia, return to you, although I don't think he ever will. He plays hockey, and thinks his Russian roots fostered this passion. He is proud of his heritage.

And I know you would be proud of what he has become. He is in his final year of high school and is off to an all boys college next year. He is kind and funny and smart. He loves to fish, play hockey and lacrosse, hang with his friends—anything active, anything outside. He can be both serious and goofy. My husband and I joke there would have been no way we could have birthed a son as inherently good as he is.

You must wonder what he looks like. That he has naturally straight teeth and has the most gorgeous smile. That he needs to shave daily and likes to lift weights. Would you want to know that we go on mother/son dates—out for dinner, to the movies? These are some of my favorite moments, and I wouldn't want to think of any other mother taking my place.

About his name—I wonder why you chose Grigory. Was it a family name? I preferred his nickname Grisha, which we held onto as a middle name. He now has a different first name, though every now and then, I call him Grisha. It seems he thinks of that as his baby name, and used to pronounce it Gree-ta. I would have forgotten all of these details had I not chronicled every bit of our journey to bring him home. Home. Yes. That is where he is now.

I am fairly certain we will never meet. We hope to take him back to Russia one day, but we're afraid. We don't trust your country's leaders. Getting him out the first time was hard enough. He knows he has two older sisters, and used to speak of them as if they lived a couple blocks over. Although I am certain he has not stopped wondering about them, he has stopped asking.

He has a brother, who is also adopted from Russia, whom I feel equally blessed, and just as proprietary about. But that is a different letter, to a different mother.

You. He has never asked about you, and it may be only to protect my feelings. I have told him everything I know about his past, which isn't much, but more than many adopted kids know.

Have you heard about the boy whose parents adopted him from Russia, with just a name and date of birth? Have you heard how well adjusted he is, without any hint of an attachment disorder? How he makes his mother laugh—and feel extremely proud—every day. How he is loved by his teachers, his family, and so many others. Have you heard?

Color-by-Number

There are details with my father that I struggle to retrieve, like the unshaded spaces in a color-by-number worksheet. Now, decades after he died, my sister says, "Don't you remember when Dad would take us to the Y and we'd hang out in that office upstairs?" I've heard about Mom being at work and how Captain Jack, the gym manager, would babysit us while Dad played handball. Our eyes would travel from our father in his pit-stained T-shirts—or were they an unmarred white—over to his huffing opponent, and through the plexiglass we'd knock and wave when either of them missed. I want to say, "Couldn't we hear the guys grunting from the weight room?" and "Didn't the place reek of dirty socks?" But I can't. Even though I was seven or eight at the time, I will never be able to fill those empty spaces.

If only there were a way to trade other child-hood memories for more with my father, to shade more spaces. Swap out the ones with the man my mother dated two years after Dad died. Erase the days after school when he'd be lurking at our house while Mom was still at work. As I turned onto Avon, I'd spot his silver truck parked in the driveway. I'd shield my eyes as the sun thrashed light off the back bumper, as fear lumped in the pit of my stomach; I never knew when he'd barge into my bedroom without knocking or when he'd start hurling trash—granola bar wrappers, emptied chip bags, his words. If only I could forget his inappropriate stares, the venom in his voice. If only I could choose the moments when childhood amnesia were to hit.

Lucky

When I was in high school my mother said I should consider myself lucky that my father had died. When I asked her what she meant, she said he would have been more strict. I was nine when he died. I never considered myself lucky. I tried to imagine how my father's death had been fortuitous. If he'd lived—even if he were as strict as they come—I wouldn't have had to worry that my mother could up and die too, that I'd be left an orphan. *You're lucky he died.* I could've forgone intense fear that we'd run out of money. *Lucky.* Forgone the embarrassment and shame that stems from being different. Why would anyone want to be friends with someone from such a sad, pitiful family? Someone so lucky.

I have written fiction based on my childhood—a character named Sally Jo represents
me. In this version, rather than have the father
die, I imagine he'd survived. Too many bad
things have happened in my life for Sally Jo's
childhood to have been much easier; in this al-
ternate universe, her parents divorce. Any version better than the truth. Any world where her
father does not die. My friend's parents divorced when we were in junior high, and she
experienced similar feelings of shame and embarrassment. I imagine the same for Sally Jo—
her parents' divorce would not be the kind
where the mother and father remain best
friends. It would not be the kind where the parents create a healthy, stable environment for
their child. Sally Jo could only be so lucky.

You're lucky. Did my mother not realize I
would have taken countless rules over lifelong
abandonment issues? His authoritarian ways
over endless fear that everyone I love will die?

My dad wasn't the best husband, and it is
possible that had he lived, my parents would
have divorced. My mother may have still dated
the same horrible man for five years, though
my father would not have allowed him to ver-
bally and emotionally abuse my sister and me
the way he had. My mother often chose her
boyfriend over us, and without a father, there
had been no other parent or adult to turn to.

You're lucky your father died. How could I feel fortunate to have lost the one person who could have protected me? My mother passed away twelve years ago and I can't tell her what needs to be said. I can't say that my father, the same man who often yelled and was strict with us, would have been equally hard on her boyfriend. It took decades of therapy to forgive my mother for allowing this horrible stranger into my life, longer for telling me I was lucky. More therapy to reconcile my need to think of her in this way.

Lucky your father died. When I was a child, there were things I needed to talk about, more than how strict my father would have been. I wanted to say how scared I was and how there was so much about my father that I didn't know. So much I will never know.

Could we start this conversation over? *You're lucky.*

Could we start with *your father died*?

Guess What's Different

(1982) If you were to stop by my childhood home on Parkview Avenue, you'd enter through the back door, into the kitchen. If my mother had been cleaning that day, you'd smell the citrusy scent of Pledge, the sting of bleach, along with the usual: bitter coffee grounds piling up in the trash. You'd fling your backpack onto the kitchen table, the rectangle one with the flaps that flipped up for "supper," as my mother called it.

If you were lucky, and it was near dusk, you might catch the last of the day's light burst through the window above the sink. Notice how the rays wrapped the stove, toaster, and broom closet in an amber thread. Look out that same window, peer at the caramel-colored sky, see how it framed the neighbors' chimneys, the jagged line of treetops, how it lit up the tele-phone wires. Grab any one of the pastel tupper-ware cups from the nearest cupboard, fill and refill the narrow glass intended for a toddler's grip.

You'd then turn right, take three steps—or two giant ones—into the dining room. Notice the stacks of my mother's nursing books scattered across the dining room table. To the left, you'd see the matching breakfast buffet, the framed photos of my sister Beth and me nestled among my mother's potted plants—the geraniums, ferns, and aloe vera.

If you were to walk straight, you'd enter the living room, the coziest area of the house. In the daytime, floor-to-ceiling windows heated up every reading spot: slumped against the book-shelf in the corner, lying flat in front of the fire-place, sinking into either end of the brown-and-orange-patterned couch. At night, when the fireplace was aflame, the room glowed and shot lively shadows across the ceiling. It smelled like earth and oak, felt safe.

If you were to turn left, you'd slip your stockinged feet down the plastic vinyl runners, past the crucifix—the one displayed at my fa-ther's funeral—and enter a hallway. Come to a halt in front of a photo collage, be drawn to a 5x7 of my father's unsmiling face. It was the photograph that had been taken for his driver's license; my mother had it blown up to fit the largest of the frame's slots. Set against the DMV's maroon backdrop, his dark eyes and pale skin stood out among the surrounding pictures; there is one of our family cat wearing a bonnet; another from Beth's First Communion—her veil asail in the wind—and one from my communion, celebrated two months after my dad died. My neighbor had taken the only photo from that day; she'd asked my mother, sister, and me to pose in the front yard, next to the maple tree. With our arms limp against our sides and flattened expressions, we stood apart. Heavy sadness needs room to breathe.

(1980) It was a Monday night in March, and my mother, Beth, and I had just returned from religion class. My sister had been sitting on one end of the couch; and, on the other, I was deep into Judy Blume's *Tales of a Fourth Grade Nothing*. I'd read it in second grade, now again in third, and planned to re-read it in the fourth. My mom sat on a separate seat. It was almost 8:00, minutes from the time she typically changed into her pajamas. She'd been watching TV, and I figured she'd been waiting for a commercial so she wouldn't miss any of *M*A*S*H*. As a nurse, she seemed to identify with the medical emergencies. "Yep, he needs to be intubated," she'd say to Major Houlihan. "Stat."

I heard three sharp raps at the door. I always got scared when anyone came to the front entrance; all of our friends and relatives entered through the side door, the one attached to the driveway. And they usually buzzed the doorbell rather than knocked.

None of us moved. They knocked again, harder this time. Even though I stayed put, my instinct was to hide, like my sister and I did whenever the Jehovah's Witnesses wandered our neighborhood. My mother usually peeked through the nearest window before opening; she didn't tonight. It was below zero, and as she yanked at the thick wooden door, the cold seeped in. My mother stepped back as two police officers filled the tiny foyer.

The heavier, older-looking one cleared his throat. "Are you the wife of Charles Henry Triemert?" I was reminded that my dad's middle name was the same as Grandpa's first. Knowing that families followed that pattern with naming, I'd always been relieved that my parents hadn't given me my mother's: LaVaune. My middle name was Jo, which wasn't much better.

My mother nodded and took another step backward. I didn't know why she hadn't answered his question. Yes, she should have said, I'm his wife.

The same officer removed his hat, held it against his chest. "I am sorry to report that tonight at 6:30 Charles died from cardiac arrest. He'd been playing handball." At 6:30, we were in the middle of religion class; he'd been alive as we entered the church's parking lot. The silent officer, the one who didn't seem to have a purpose, bowed his head. Days later I would wonder why policemen were the ones designated to deliver this news. Arresting bad guys, pulling over speeding drivers—wasn't that enough?

My mother returned to her chair: the velvet one with the soft golden arms. Into it, she dropped. I scurried off to her side, tucked beneath her arm. My sister followed and squeezed in on her left. I went to embrace my mother—I felt like that was what someone in my situation should do—and could feel the warm tears on her face, hear her soft whimpers.

We sat there for several minutes, entwined. One of the officers must have turned down the volume on the TV—I saw what looked like laughter escape from the mouths of Hawkeye and Radar.

(1984) If you were to enter my house, you would see the new cabinets that my mother's boyfriend Randy had made. Stained in dark wood, they had clear handles that encased a variety of beans: kidney, pinto, lima, and black-eyed peas. A collection to showcase stunted growth. You wouldn't see any light in the room—and wouldn't for the five years they dated—because Randy had installed new blinds and liked them to be shut. Sunlight, he said, caused him migraines. If you were to open the fridge, you couldn't miss the rows of beer bottles and fancy cheeses that had replaced the Velveeta and bologna; and next to the microwave, you'd see the new wine rack—each slot had been filled.

If you were to walk into the dining room, you'd notice the vinyl runners had been removed, and on the new green carpet, spot the lined markings from a vacuum cleaner. The dining room table had been covered with white linen, and my mother's nursing books had been moved to a nearby chair. If it were near dinner time—no longer called supper—the table would be set with the rarely used polished silverware and decorative plates. A single candle would be lit.

Randy had never been formally introduced to Beth and me—he showed up two years after my father died. I thought he'd been hired to remodel our kitchen. Before I realized they were a couple, he'd been given keys to our house. While my mother was at work—and before Randy started to let himself in—my sister and

I'd had free rein; we'd eat Ho Hos standing at the counter, one after another, play video games for way too long, and discard our jackets and school uniforms wherever we felt.

Now, we'd neatly line up our shoes on the stairs leading to the basement and hang our coats and backpacks on the hook behind the back door. Randy had given that hook to my mother on Valentine's Day. He'd purchased it on their trip to the North Shore; it had two loons gazing longingly at one another and the inscription read: "R.F. loves L.T." It made me feel nauseous, but because of how much of a neatfreak Randy was, I felt pressured to use it. As I entered the back door, I could hear the wind escape from the vacuum cleaner and the screech of its wheels as Randy rolled it back into the front closet. He never said hello, and in his presence I used as few words as possible.

He stood in the kitchen doorway, its edges framing his tall slender build. I tried not to look at his lumpy red face, silver-blue eyes, and dark, peppery hair. "Could you make your bed before your ma comes home?"

Why'd he been in my bedroom? I had that door shut for a reason.

I nodded, one quick tip, barely noticeable, just so he couldn't report back that I'd been ignoring him. Before I made my way to my bedroom, I grabbed a snack-sized bag of Cheetos and a box of granola bars. I shut my door and billowed my afghan over my bed, disguising the mess beneath. My mother never used to care much about cleanliness—she only seemed to mind when company was coming. Now she too was obsessed.

Each week, when Friday night came around, Randy would say, "Don't you have any plans?" He'd lift his eyebrows in a creepy way. "No friends to hang out with?" I was in seventh grade, and most of my friends were homebodies, too.

One Friday night near Christmas, Randy told my mother they were going out for drinks and dancing. At school that day, I'd been looking forward to making sugar cookies; I was hoping my mother would want to help, but I didn't expect much. I figured Randy would be over, and he'd want her all to himself. When I baked cookies, I liked to add a personal touch—sometimes I'd add flaked coconut, dried cranberries, Reese's Pieces, whatever I could find. "Less is more," my mother would remind me. "*Way* less."

I was seated at the kitchen table, all of my ingredients laid out before me—I hadn't yet decided what to add. On their way out, my mother followed Randy into the kitchen. Her new perfume, spicier than usual, led the way. Soft curls wisped against her forehead and neck, and her red lipstick and rosy blush made her look young, happy. Randy, I thought, was a lucky man.

"Honey, please don't add too many ingredients," she said. "You know what I always say."

I smiled up at her. "Less is more," I whispered.

She leaned down to kiss the top of my head. "We'll be back around 10. I love you," she said.

"I don't," Randy said, extra loud.

My mother giggled, as if it were the most hilarious joke she'd ever heard.

Once the door shut behind them, I went and found my backpack, dug to the bottom and scooped up stale conversation hearts from Valentine's Day. Found some Christmas cookie decorations in the back of the cabinet: green and white confection beads and Redhots meant for Rudolph's nose. I smashed granola bars— added all of that and everything I'd already laid out.

I added ingredients until the white dough was no longer white.

Kept adding until the cookies were sure to be ruined.

(2008) If you were to enter my childhood home, you'd notice the return of light. The aluminum blinds had been replaced with thin wooden ones, and they were always open. The cabinets had been re-stained a lighter shade and the seed handles had been replaced with simple, standard knobs. You might be surprised to see that the loon hook was still behind the door even though my mother hadn't dated Randy for twenty years. Open the fridge, and you'd notice a beer bottle here or there, not the rows of reserves.

As you walked into the dining room, you might miss that the carpet had been removed, allowing the original wooden floor to shine through. The dining room table had been replaced by a hospital bed. The nursing books? She was forced to retire months ago.

My mother would be lying there; two days after I'd returned from Russia to meet my younger son, she'd been diagnosed with terminal brain cancer. Now six months later, live-in caretakers had been hired and my mother had been confined to her bed.

Toward the end, the cancer had eaten much of her cognitive skills and she acted like a child. At times, it was hard to distinguish between the behavior of my mother and that of Mitch, my six-year-old son.

Three days before she died, when she communicated only through moans and never opened her eyes, I got a call from my aunt.

"Your mother is awake and asking for French toast."

"Wait, she's talking?" I said. The French toast part did not surprise me.

"Yep, your sister is on her way."

I was shocked—I picked Mitch up from camp and drove over.

My son had been learning games at camp. "Guess What's Different" was his favorite. Someone in the group would leave the room and then return after having changed something about their appearance.

The first couple of rounds were normal. Mitch left the room and came back with his socks folded over. My sister walked into the bathroom and returned with her shorts pockets turned inside out. Each time we allowed my son to be the one to give the correct answer. The rest made guesses.

"You grew a beard?" said one aunt.

"You finally combed your hair?" from my sister.

"You took a bath?"

When it was my third or fourth turn, I was running out of things to change. I went into the den, my old bedroom, and put my underwear on over my shorts. I walked out.

"You put on some lipstick?" another aunt said.

My sister raised her eyebrows. "You ironed your shirt?"

"You guys really don't know?" Mitch's eyes widened.

By this time we'd formed teams, and my son was on mine. He was bouncing up and down in his chair, unable to contain his excitement over our possible lead.

My mother was laughing so hard, the last great laugh of her life.

Three days later, she'd be gone.

(Now) If you were to walk into my mother's home, there would be little trace of her. The photos had long since been replaced, the floors restained, the nursing books and dining room table had been sent to the Goodwill, had found new homes.

A few years after my mother died, my sister and I were in our old neighborhood. New owners had since moved in, a young couple, and we'd heard from friends that the wife was pregnant. A new cycle. We knocked on the back door and explained who we were, told them that we'd lived at this house for our entire childhoods. We asked if we could look around; the woman seemed reluctant, but eventually let us in. I entered through the back door, expected scents of coffee and cleaning. Nothing. I walked down the hallway, through the dining room—all of the furniture was modern, neutral, foreign— and they were turning my old bedroom into a nursery. They were having a boy.

On my way out, I craned my neck behind the door. There hung the loon hook. I could imagine Randy standing near that spot, the day I'd ruined the cookies. I shuffled my feet, coughed, jiggled the door handle, my keys—anything to drown out the echo of his laughter, petulant and mocking. But, because this is my imagination, mine, my mother tells him to knock it off, shoves him out the door. Of course, she follows him—I can only expect so much—though this time around, she does not laugh.

What I Could Never Say
To My Mother's Boyfriend

It wasn't because you shipped all of my toys out to the garage that I wished you dead.

Gone were the chalkboard I used to play school, the bright pink tea set, my Barbie Dreamhouse—tossed like trash next to the shovels and metal garbage cans. Eleven years old and grieving the death of my father, gone but two years. Fear and sorrow had been nipping at my innocence—you yanked at what was left. Trapped in adult emotions, I needed those toys to keep me young. My mother forced you to haul them back inside. Touched by your rough hands, your angry heart, I never played with them again.

Sunburn

After Mom died we had been set aside like socks that no longer matched. For us to fit into the lives of others, must my sister and I come with a mother? Like an admittance ticket, or our way to lease a portion of their thoughts? I'd been picking away at the layers of sadness, like the days following a sunburn, peeling back skin and scab. Remember the burn that painted us crimson red, as we basked beside Lake Josephine on the most overcast of days? Wrong were we to think the clouds would protect us. Mom had been gone, and we were left to grieve alone—to furrow our way through the silence, the longing for our mother's laugh, her dainty embraces, simple Sunday night dinners at the Thai place where the service was horrible but the food was never too spicy.

One cannot protect a cloud from the sharp winds—nor can a prayer make someone love you.

Snapshot at Gatorland

There on my nightstand stood a neon pink picture frame—the enclosed photograph had been taken by my mother at an alligator reserve. In the picture, my father, with his sideburns and bushy 80s mustache, is pitching patches of leaves to the reptiles while several peacocks have craned their necks to watch. Although my sister and I are in the picture, we're not standing near him, nor facing him.

After my father died when I was nine, my mother didn't have to say that my sister and I weren't allowed to talk about him. We obeyed the tears pooling in the corners of her eyes, the quiver in her upper lip, the reddening around her nose. With few pictures of the two of us—and even fewer words—the photo from Gatorland dictated my memories. How could one image capture how much Beth and I had looked forward to Florida, spending time with our father, our first ride on an airplane? Or how, upon arrival, the dull sky shone a mysterious haze of black. That night the warm, sticky breeze seeped through my clothes—the air smelled like winter jasmine and freshly cut grapefruit. "Can we *finally* see the ocean?" Beth and I chirped from the back seat. Other than an eight-foot-long pool shoved against the highway, our motel was nowhere near water.

As we pulled into the parking lot, I could hear the crash of the evening waves, the palm trees crinkling in the wind, imagined seahorses and sand dollars scattered along the shoreline. A tantalizing, tongue-twisting panorama. Beth and I kicked off our shoes and sprinted down the sloping sand, toward the darkness. The salty air spread through my long, tangled hair, and the sand bit at the bottoms of my feet. My father cupped his chilled January hands, hollered, "Slow down," although his comments didn't seem meant for me. Unconvinced the ocean tasted like salt, I trailed my hand through the icy water, licked my fingertips. My father clapped as my sister did backflip after backflip across the moist sand, slapping and shooting in and out of the waves. Wet, dry, wet, dry—we were in a trance.

The next day, before the sun cleared the horizon, my father had left for a business meeting. My mother, sister, and I hung out at the motel. Dad worked long hours at home; this felt no different.

"Marco," I said to my sister as I shot across the pool.

As if she could detect my location through her fingers, Beth waved her hands through the air. "Polo."

Our mother basked poolside, her long, tidy body wrapped in a brown-and-white bikini. Fancy, she looked, sipping a can of Coke through a straw. Fancy, too, as she crossed and recrossed her pedicured toes, as she sorted through the fanned magazines on the cement beside her. I like to think she'd been imagining we were at The Four Seasons, not a motor inn.

"Mom, can you judge our handstand contest?" I said. "We need someone to time us."

She propped her nose above her copy of *Redbook*. "Sure."

Beth went first. With slim ankles that brushed up against one another, pointed toes and arched ballerina's feet, hers was beautiful. Nineteen one thousand, I counted along to myself.

My mom waited for my sister to resurface: "Six seconds. Not bad." Beth hung her head.

"C'mon Mom." I squinted toward my mother. I knew she hadn't been paying attention and told her to put the magazine down.

My mother dog-eared a page, let out a sigh. Beth went again. Moments later, I noticed my mother had been sneaking peeks, now of *Good Housekeeping*. She shook her head. "Fine." She stretched the magazine open wide and gently laid it on a nearby lawn chair. "Only one more contest though," she said.

After we talked her into judging our somersault and pencil dives, too, Beth and I swam until we'd pruned our fingertips and pinkened our cheeks and noses. My father had taken the rental car, so when our growling stomachs were too loud to ignore, we made our way to the nearest roadside diner where we ate grilled cheese sandwiches and chicken strips.

After swimming again at the pool, we trudged back to the same restaurant for French fries and chocolate shakes. Although the same waitress was still working, she didn't serve us again, but took time to drop off pennies for us to buy gumballs from the machine by the front door. Though I felt special, I now wonder if the waitress felt sorry for us, for the two girls who had eaten twice at the same roadside diner, who spoke in breathless bursts of their missing father.

Back at the motel, before falling asleep, Beth and I flicked through the channels and caught glimpses of R-rated movies, of all their blood, skin, and rage. My mother was too tired to notice, and my dad, if he'd been there, would have asked us to turn the TV off, but only to avoid the likelihood of us wrestling him awake later on with our nightmares.

I startled when he shuffled in.

"Chuck, they won't stop talking about it." She waved a brochure in the air. In the lobby, my sister had found the ad—glossy and colorful and covered with reptiles.

"Do we have to? I'm beat." He softened his voice. "Can't we just hang by the pool?"

"No ifs, ands, or buts about it," she said. "We're going." I'd only mentioned Gatorland once; perhaps she'd been the one who was most interested.

As the morning sun barged its way into our motel room, my father woke first, shook on his pants, and grabbed his wallet. "Can I come?" I asked, guessing he wanted coffee. Before he even agreed, I'd slipped out of bed and snuck through the door before it clicked shut. He may have hoped to sneak out unnoticed, to allow for some down time before the big day ahead; if he had, he didn't let on. Like most children, I grounded myself in the moment, with only a murky awareness of anything, anybody else.

He found free coffee in the lobby and let me peel back the tin creamers, pour in the silken ribbons of white. "Want anything?" He'd pointed to the vending machine. I chose plain M&M's even though I didn't want any. My mother would not allow candy before breakfast—I figured this would be our secret. He'd always been less strict when it came to nutrition (and cleaning and homework and bed times).

We sat on lawn chairs beside the pool. I rested my elbows on the wobbly table between us. "Dad, wanna do cannonballs with me later?"

He looked distracted, but then turned to me and smiled. "Yep, Grace, sure thing." Grace, his nickname for me. Grace, of which I had none.

"Dad, when I get back to school will I have a lot of homework to make up? Dad, do you think Tricia will invite me to her party? I mean, I didn't invite her to mine but I only invited four friends and when you only invite four friends—"

He nodded along, occasionally checking his watch. I kept chatting as long as he would allow.

When my mother and sister woke and found us by the pool, I knew my time with my father was gone. It was time to map out our day. Once we figured out Gatorland didn't open for over an hour, Dad agreed to drive past the ocean. We didn't want to waste time at the diner, so we ate breakfast ordered from a McDonald's drive-thru. Scanning Disney and SeaWorld billboards through the backseat windows, we nibbled on greasy egg sandwiches and sipped on cartons of pulpy orange juice. My parents listened to the radio and spoke about the weather, the traffic, whether or not we were lost. My mother said they spoke of my father's health during this trip, but I never noticed. I wonder if the heart attack that stole his life could've been prevented if he'd taken his symptoms seriously and, instead of going to Gatorland, we'd driven to the hospital.

When we reached the same beach we'd seen the night before, once again Beth and I tossed off our sandals and darted toward the coastline. We stopped. Filled with seaweed and dirty foam, the water was not the seahorses and sand dollars I'd imagined. Even though my father explained that things looked a little different in the daytime, I couldn't believe I'd scooped this same water into my mouth. Though confused about the state of the water, whatever my father said was the truth, and I didn't question him further. I never questioned him about much: his need to work endless hours, why he had to hit the gym *every* night, his absence at church and school events, why he never attended my birthday parties.

I scan the photo now. If we'd looked happy, or had merely been standing near one another, perhaps I would've remembered my time with him differently. I wish his last photo could have been from our time at the beach—the first night, when everything seemed safe and simple—or during our private moments by the pool. If we'd known how things would turn out, we might have staged this picture and linked arms. We may have stood near one another to suggest we were part of a unit. Perhaps, that is only wishful thinking, from those who know the ending.

Interwoven Foliage

It was the last image of my father, taken at a reptile zoo in the middle of Florida. I continue to search the photograph for whatever I may have missed. As if I'd overlooked a charcoal-coated osprey lurking behind a branch or the jagged shell of a reptile egg rubbing against my father's shoe. If I look close—squint through the fingerprint smudges and past the tired edges—I might find what's not visible to the naked eye. The scaly auburn bark freeing itself from a longleaf pine; or the delicate, lavender blossoms of the beautyberry. And by that shrub, spot the speckled wings of a swallowtail, a native butterfly slurping up its sweet nectar. Further back, notice the interwoven foliage: the firebush and spiderwort and silver buttonwood, tangled, strangling out the light.

I'd once committed to memory what the picture captured: the way my father pitched patches of leaves to the alligators, dark and menacing, like a harbinger of his death. Had memorized the way a bevy of dazzling and vibrant peacocks appear to be closing in on him. Perched precariously, he was, between light and darkness, life and death. Weeks later, he'd be gone. I continue to scan the photograph, expecting new details to emerge. Hunt, too, for what the photo could never reveal: my father's inner dialogue, what he was most proud of, his biggest fears. Had it been to die? Had it been to leave his family so soon?

Names Have Been Changed

Shot, Shot, Shot, Joe chants when his college roommate walks in.

My boyfriend Joe bought his first house, and we are ready to celebrate. Within the hour, a plastic cup of red wine spills, and bleeds its way deathly close to a white rug. His twin brother stacks a pyramid of empty Budweiser cans inside the garter snake's cage. After I slam a few Screwdrivers, the party becomes a blur of broken lamps and hearts, tear-induced laughter, and drunk girls cackling down in the basement. Just before 3:00 a.m., I hear mating calls from the spare bedroom and spot a guy snuggling up to a decorative pillow in the bathtub.

Joe and I fall into bed, and my head spins on the pillow. I wake to gray and plaid shadows, the sheen of a wristwatch. I hear the tinny sound of a mattress coil before I see what looks like Kirk, Joe's friend from his bartending days, toppling off the foot of the bed. I recall images of Kirk—seconds earlier—trying to jam his hand down the front of my half-zipped pants. I rub my eyes as I try to make sense of it all. I had been lying next to my boyfriend, had felt safe enough to feel the electric heat of his body, to inhale his dank, boozy breath.

I rattle Joe awake, and he tumbles back to sleep. I tiptoe into the next room. Kirk appears to be asleep in the La-Z-boy, with his mouth hanging open—he looks like a baby turkey vulture. I stare at his half-open mouth, imagine drool dripping from his hungry upper lip. I want to shake him, turn on the lights, wake the whole damn house, ask: Why, Why, Why?

I stop. *Have I dreamt this whole thing*? A side effect of my antidepressants is that they heighten the sexuality in my dreams.

I slip back into the bedroom, shake my boyfriend harder this time. I insist that he go and check. I tell him that Kirk is faking, that he's not asleep. Joe moans and sighs as he is ripped awake, as I tell him what happened, about the thud on the carpeting. A water cup knocks to the ground, an overhead light buzzes on, the mattress bows as he scooches out. I follow Joe to the next room, still wondering if I'd been dreaming—I did increase my dose of meds.

Kirk is no longer in the chair. Joe walks to the front door. Soft flurries had collected on the mounds of hard, stubborn snow. He checks for footprints in the fresh flakes—reports there hadn't been any. No freshly grooved tire tracks either.

Later that day, Joe calls. How could you be so sure? he says. Your drugs make you crazy.

I bite my lip. Know he is done listening.

Before hanging up, he adds, I'd never be friends with someone who would do something like that.

I imagine going to my psychiatrist later in the week, to inquire about the drug's side effects. Was it possible, I'd ask, that I'd imagined it all?

Flinch as the doctor grazes his hand over an exposed knee, across a sleeveless shoulder, and tells me it's all in my head.

Explosive Orchids

When the brown beehive of hair bobbled your way, you knew you were in trouble. Up until then you'd been dodging adult attention: the stares, the hugs—some clumsy and loose, others rib-crushing and breathless. Avoidance is hard when it's your father's wake and you are nine. The coned hairdo belonged to Mrs. Leitner, your kindergarten teacher. You did not expect to see her here. She had always yelled at the class, screamed at you. When you could not back away any further, she said. "It's time to say goodbye to your father." Up until then, everything had been dull and fuzzy, as if peering through rain-soaked glass. When she grabbed your wrist with her bony, taloned fingers, you were jolted into awareness. Could now see detail in the path you were being dragged, see the ironed creases in the men's trousers, see the glint of a penny someone must have dropped, see the suntanned tint of shiny nylon-ed legs, see the wrinkled-up kleenex Aunt Linda had been dabbing at her nose, now held limp by her side. Could hear the priest's booming voice, "too young to die," the whispered condolences, "heart attack," the nervous laughter from your older cousins, hear "he was only forty-two, "and "those poor girls."

You were now six feet from the casket, and Mrs. Leitner was not letting up. All you could see was the tip of your father's nose, the same nose everyone said you had. You had his eyes. Mouth, too. Some said you'd shared his sense of humor, others: his mischievous side. Suddenly, the smell of the peace lilies and orchids were explosive and almost spun you back into a cloud of dizziness. Or was it blissful oblivion? You dug your heels into the ground. Though the shag carpeting was slippery and your patent leathers couldn't gain traction. Skidding on a patch of ice, it felt—with no rail to grab onto, no support. You shifted your weight, stretched out your arms, grasped at the air for balance. You didn't say to Mrs. Leitner what you wanted. Didn't say: *This is the last place I want to be. My father's dead face is not something I want to remember.* Didn't say: *No one invited you, so why are you here*? Didn't say: *No one in my family even liked you, especially my father.* Nor did you say, *When you die, I will never attend your funeral.* Instead, you drove your heels in more, made divots in the carpeting. Floated back into your safety net of distraction and escape, back where none of this had happened, where everyone was alive and well, where your greatest worry was whether you received an A or an A- on your spelling quiz. You were not moving forward, not here, not for your former teacher, not for anyone. There was one more similarity she may not have known. Stubborn you were, like your father.

Button-stitch

According to Mrs. Jorgenson, the religion teacher, our First Communion dresses had to be white or ivory and swing just below the knee. Most of the girls bought theirs off a rack at a department store, but my mother made ours—my older sister's and mine. She brought us along to Jo-Ann Fabrics, allowed us time to browse, to lay our hands on the bolts of fabric: the velvets and satins and thick cottons. Some were soft, others starchy and crisp.

As I trailed my fingers across one piece of cloth, my hand stalled. I was drawn to its imprinted shapes, raised borders, the rhythm of its pattern. With the pads of my index finger and thumb, I pressed at one of the cut-out ovals—tap, tap, tap—swirled my fingertip over the rim of the opening. Imagined I was dipping a feather's tip in ink.

"Eyelet," my mother whispered, as her hand glossed over it. Her voice steeled: "Grandma used to call it button-stitch." From our moment, she had been ripped away—my mother was never as close to her own. She softened, and said, "It's beautiful."

We didn't call it button-stitch; to us, it was "eyelet." So subtle on the lips. "Eyelet," like whispering "lilac," and "hyacinth," or any delicate flower.

At home, I'd peek over my mother's shoulder as she tinkered with her sewing kit, as she stretched and admired her handiwork. She let me shake out the patterned tissue paper, double-check her measurements, trace the dotted lines with my finger tip. But when she turned on the sewing machine, she vanished. Hypnotized by the steady beat of the needle, the feel of the fabric as it slid between her fingers. Cocooned, she was, in her seamstress trance.

***

When my father did not come home from work, two months before my Communion, my mother became cocooned in her sadness. My sister and I were put on hold. She needed to plan a funeral.

I wore the navy blue velvet dress I'd worn for picture day to my father's funeral. To stave off temptation, she'd stored the white patent leathers she'd bought to match my communion dress on the top shelf of her closet. The night before the funeral she set the pair on my dresser, still shiny in their original box, with their artificial scent of plastic and cardboard. It seemed she was no longer concerned that I'd scuff them up. It was true—so much of our pre-served lives had already been scuffed.

She didn't turn on the sewing machine in the weeks following the funeral either. I watched my dress lay abandoned, breathless, on a nearby table. I overheard her on the phone, talking with a friend. "I don't know how I'm go-ing to do this." Do what, I wondered. Finish my dress? Figure out a way to pay our bills? En-sure my sister and I are cared for and feel safe?

"How is my dress coming along?" I said later that night, in a playful way, in an attempt to buoy her back to her light-hearted self. "Need me to help?"

When she smiled without showing her teeth—and without any crease in the skin around her eyes—I knew to stop.

On the morning of my Communion, I woke early. My mother said she'd heat up the curling iron after breakfast. For the funeral, I'd worn ponytails, but she promised she'd style it today.

I walked into the kitchen with my dress zipped two inches from the top. "Mom, can you help—"

In front of the stove, my mother—still wearing her pajamas and ratty slippers—shook her head. "Not to breakfast." She tilted her chin away, flipped a pancake. The sizzle lingered in my ears.

"Could I cover it with a towel?" I asked. Like we did to prevent stains on picture day.

As her shoulders slouched, her body deflated. I slunk back to my room to change. I slipped off my dress, and left it in a heap on the rug.

My mother skipped breakfast—she said she needed to figure out what my sister was going to wear. Alone at the kitchen table, I stabbed chunks of pancake, drowned the buttery bits in syrup, could barely swallow because it was all too soggy, too sweet. At the same time, tasteless.

After eating, I kicked my piled-up gown off the floor; re-dressing felt like a chore. When I returned to the kitchen—this time with my shoes, tights, and veil on—I expected her to ooh and aww, say I resembled a princess, like she had said to my sister on her Communion Day.

"Go check if the iron is hot," she said. "I need to do my own hair first."

With my father's funeral just weeks behind us, I shouldn't have expected her to be bouncing around the house. But I did want the day to be centered around me. I am sure she, too, couldn't fathom celebrating anything in the same church that had just held my father's funeral. I had once planned to parade down the walkway, like my sister had done, to flaunt my dress and veil. Now it seemed unimaginable to walk down the aisle—the exact cement tiles—that my father's dead body had been carried down weeks earlier.

Once my mother, sister and I were dressed and headed to the car, Leone, our elderly neighbor, appeared in our front yard. "Wait." She lifted her voice to reach us across the yard. "Let's get a family photo." Her request was disorienting; the definition of "family" had changed.

She ordered us to pose opposite the maple tree, on the sun-drenched side of the yard. Child. ~~Parent~~. Parent Child. Our new lineup. I couldn't help but think of my father's vacant spot, and my thoughts remained on him as I passed by the front door. Two months earlier, police officers had arrived, and stood right there on *those* steps, knocked on *that* wooden door. That evening my sister and I tucked ourselves into our winter coats and were shuffled from our living room into the back of a squad car. Like criminals, as if we were to blame for our heartbreak. The police drove us the three miles to my grandparents' house—my dad's parents. In every way, my mother's own family had always been more distant.

"I love Susie's dress," Leone said in the direction of my mother.

"Susie picked out the fabric. Button-stitch," my mother said. I mouthed "eyelet," as my gaze drifted back to the wooden door, to my father.

As Leone snapped the photo, a light breeze picked up and twirled the crowns of my mother's rose bushes, rustled the leaves of her ferns. It was a little before nine, too early for the heat and humidity to swell and stagnate the air. Some god somewhere knew we needed something—a little wind, some movement. A reprieve.

This morning, we had assigned seats. Mine was in a pew that was a few back from the front, the same pew in which I'd sat for the funeral. I took my place nearest the aisle, like all of the other Communion candidates.

Two rows ahead of me, across the aisle, sat Jenny Krider. We had been in the same first grade class, been born on the same day, and lived three blocks apart. Her brother looked exactly like their father, and Jenny looked like her mother, who was pretty, younger than the other moms, and could roller skate better than people half her age.

During the Our Father, Mrs. Krider flattened one of Jenny's wayward curls and inched her daughter's veil to the right. I imagined her mother whispering, "There, honey, you look like an angel." Mrs. Krider beamed downward. I glanced up to see my mother staring ahead, her face vacant.

I grazed my hand over the fabric of my gown, became entranced by the pattern. For a moment, I escaped.

During a lull in the service, I leaned over to my mother. "Could you fix my veil? I think it's come loose." I lied, but I wanted to feel as important as Jenny Krider.

My mother sighed, as if I'd asked her to get up and take over for the priest. She put her stiff hand on my veil and shoved it. The combs on the veil's crown dug deep into my head. I didn't adjust them. Had finally felt something other than numbness and emptiness. It was pain, physical pain. And it felt something like relief.

Childhood Amnesia

Just as the sun peeks between the maple's branches and light has crept its way in through the wooden blinds, my son crawls into my bed. "Remember when we swam in the pool with Uncle Tom," Mitch says, as he lies on his stomach next to me. "And then he threw me over his shoulders and I made that big splash?"

We had been swimming the day before; it'd be impossible to forget.

I rub his warm back. "Yes, wasn't that fun?" He turns his head away, adjusts his head on the pillow, and pretends to fall back to sleep.

"Remember when we went out for ice cream after and I got that huge sundae, and they gave me three cherries?"

Speaking in unbridled bursts and asking if I remembered was my four-year-old's way to reminisce about the week—or something that happened even a few hours earlier. Any moment he wanted to relive.

When my son is six, my mother dies, and I worry that he will forget her. Babushka, he calls his grandmother. After my dad died when I was nine, any mention of him was off limits. Perhaps this is why there's so little of him I can remember—no one had tried to etch those moments into my cache of memories. To guard them from modified narratives and the mind's inaccuracies. I needed someone to help me remember.

At night, I sit on the edge of my son's bed while I tuck him in. He is now eight. "Do you remember when Babushka took you to Como Town and let you go on as many rides as you wanted?"

The headlights of the cars outside shoot through the window and steamroll across his bed—beams run from the footies of his Spiderman jammies up to his neck and settle on his attentive stare. I see those memories dazzle in his eyes. Perhaps he pictures the two of them rounding the carousel, playing Skee-Ball, ordering cotton candy.

"And then you got your face painted to look like a tiger?" Mitch stalls on that image. We both do.

He shakes his head, dusts off any gravity. "That Babushka," he says, mimicking the tone and tempo of my speech. "She sure liked to spoil me."

Again and again, I will repeat these stories. I will not allow him to forget.

After his younger brother bounces into the back seat, Mitch sinks into the front. We are headed to his first day of high school. Though they have not kept in touch, I wonder what his relatives back in Russia recall. Had they kept track of his grade each September, as the temperatures drop, when expectations rise and fall with the weather?

Mitch was only three when we adopted him, but I'd hoped he'd retain some details of his homeland. We celebrated his third birthday there, at the orphanage, which doubled as his farewell party—goodbye to the caretakers, *paka* to his friends there, so long to living in the same city as his birth family. I tried to guard this memory against childhood amnesia.

Like breadcrumbs, I'd drop daily reminders.

"Wasn't it funny when the translator gave you a teddy bear and Elena tried to steal it?"

He nodded.

"And then you sang along to the accordion music and danced with your friends?"

Reminders, until being a high schooler steals his willingness to listen, and his memories become molded through photographs—that image on film, like a prism reflecting rays to color his thoughts. He stares at one picture, at the crazy red curls of a caretaker as she stretches and pulls at the accordion. A curious glance at the boy in denim overalls, wearing a polka-dotted party hat, dangling a deflated balloon. That boy will soon board an airplane to a faraway land, dreams and hopes fed to him by the caretakers, like fairytales and other unknowns.

My son scoots into the booth of our breakfast nook, flashes me one of his magnetic grins. Toward the end of summer, the days tick by faster. He is now headed off to college.

"I know I already told you, but when you were little you would bite your lip, shake your fists, and stomp your feet—all at the same time." This is how I introduce a memory I want to relive.

"I know, Mom. It was when I got excited, and we all said I'd become 'crazy boy.'"

Utter joy is what "crazy boy" looked like. Mitch had only been home from Russia for a month when "crazy boy" emerged; for him to feel secure enough to express himself in this way was all we wanted. We were his family; he felt safe because he knew he belonged. No matter how hard I've tried, I can't forget the full year it took to bring him home––the four trips to visit, the dreaded goodbyes, unsure if the judge would ever approve the adoption. I feared he would never belong to us. I am reminded of this now as he heads off for school; it feels eerily similar to that year of separation and anxiety–memories I don't want to relive.

Weeks after he moves into the college dorms, he keeps in contact and invites us to visit. The calls are light, even whimsical. Even though he doesn't become "crazy boy" anymore, not in the same way, I still detect versions of this secure, exuberant boy. "Crazy boy" can be heard in his chipper voice when he tells us about his new friends. About the time the kids on his floor described him as looking like a married man with three kids because of his old man's undershirts and full beard.

Two months in and a Covid outbreak sends him home. College cannot be what any of us wanted for him–he is not creating the memories his dad and I had promised. Rather than erase bits of Russia–like the sweet caretaker with the long fan of hair who gave him extra hugs, or the long drive to sightsee at Lake Baikal when he squealed, "*Machina! Machina!*" at every vehicle we passed–can we choose to forget *now*? Erase the absence of last year's lacrosse season, which would have been his first year on varsity, or the canceled spring break trip, the one he'd planned with his best friend, a boy he met his first day in America?

I hope the world can soon return to normal, so he can experience the carefree independence of college—twenty people packed into a dorm room, drawn-out cafeteria meals spent spying on crushes, last-minute road trips. So he can create more memories that bear the innocence of his time with Babushka, more starring "crazy boy." If only we could choose when childhood amnesia were to hit.

Matroyshka Dolls

1. (Ah-DEEN)

We are driving home from soccer practice, and my older son, Mitch, sits quietly, pensively, in the back seat. He catches my eye in the rearview mirror. *Matthew said he's a Swede. Mom, are we Swedes?* After I clarify that he hadn't said sweet, which his friend Matthew is not, I'm once again reminded that my son is adopted, that I hadn't given birth to either of my Russian-born children. Mitch has also momentarily forgotten, as he's done before, and we are now in that hazy limbo where I can pretend he's biologically mine. Here, I've always known him, had cared for him as an infant. An undefined, beautiful limbo. *Yes*, I want to say, *I'm part Swedish, so you are too.* Instead, I find myself saying, *Most likely not, honey, although it's possible.* I do not elaborate right away. Your blood is not mine.

2. (Dvah)

No one would disagree that bunking next to Jack is a challenge. We call him a squirmy worm. Before you know it he'll have flipped over, his toes will be skimming the headboard, and it will feel like he is trying to rappel down your side. *When I was a baby*, he asks, *was I a squirmy worm in your tummy too?* I want to say, *Yes, that was exactly how you were.* I'd go on, *You tickled my belly and I giggled for nine months straight.* He, too, forgets he is adopted, and I feel obligated to remind him. *Remember how you have a Russian mama?* I say, thinking of the title we'd given his birth mother. *I bet you squirmed all around inside her belly.* Would it have been terrible to pretend, just this once, that I knew the answer, that he indeed squirmed? There are worse things than to act as if he'd always been mine.

3. (tree)

A close friend was over for dinner when Mitch crawled onto my lap. She looked over at us and nodded. *You two look related*, she said. Although I knew what she meant, and knew she meant no harm, I wanted to say, firmly, *We are related*. I said nothing at the time. Later, I told her that although I knew her intentions were good, comments like that might confuse

Mitch. It definitely had stirred up doubt and in-security in me.

My husband and I have been completely open with our children about their adoptions. Because Mitch was two when we met him, fully aware that we hadn't always been his parents, we'd been introduced to him, not as Mom and Dad, but John and Susan. At home, we speak freely of our sons' shared heritage and repeat stories of our multiple trips to visit them in Siberia. We've preserved their Russian names, used now as middle ones. Matroyshka dolls and other Russian trinkets are displayed in nearly every room. *Are we Swedes?* We are not trying to hide anything, I remind myself.

4. (che-TYH-ree)

Even if I wanted to, it would be hard for me to forget my children are adopted. I am always reminded: at the doctor's office, filling out sports forms, worrying about their health histories, Mother's Day, speaking of their births, celebrat-ing birthdays. And not seeing my face in either of theirs. When a woman mentions her preg-nancy or the challenges she'd faced parenting an infant, I often immediately disclose my chil-dren are adopted and I can't relate; Jack was adopted at eighteen months and Mitch when he was nearly three. When people tell me my sons, who are not biologically related either, look alike or resemble me, I disclose—or remind those who have forgotten—the similarities are simply coincidental. What harm would be done if I were to nod and smile? If I were to just keep quiet when someone assumes I, too, battled morning sickness and a grueling labor. If I, like them, had been woken multiple times a night to screaming babies and multiple feedings. Those were the days, I'd think, with a smirk.

Since I'm proud of the way my family was formed, what do I hope to gain? Perhaps, I want others to see us as more united, to see them as all mine. *Was I a squirmy worm in your tummy*? Here, in this limbo, I'd have felt them grow, been the first to see their angry, red birthing faces, heard their first screams. In a way, I feel like I deserve to have been privy to all that since I am the one who cares for them now. There are moments of their lives I will never know, which seems unfair since I know them better than anyone else.

5. (pyat')

Maybe I simply want to elongate the time spent in that nebulous, beautiful limbo. To pretend, the same way my youngest does. *That Russian lady*, Jack says, *well she tried to save me from a fire. It's sad she didn't make it, but she did get me out alive.* Weeks later, he'll say,

144

That Russian lady did not survive the sinking ship. I tried to protect her, but I could only make it to shore myself. He pretends: to fill in the blanks, to control the uncontrollable, to have a say in something in which he has had none. Maybe that's all I am doing, with my idea of a hazy limbo, my pocket-sized bit of control.

Was I a squirmy worm in your tummy?

Are we Swedes?

Of course, I think, as I say, *It's possible.*

Happy Holidays to our friends and Family! 2021 has reminded us of all our blessings. Please enjoy our year in review!

Bread! So much fresh sourdough, banana bread, so many carbs! Yum! Of course we packed on some

LB's The Covid Ten hit us all! Those pounds kept us warm as we continued to exercise outside, and it didn't matter since we wore only sweatpants for our

Endless zoom calls. The exhaustion it caused, in addition to cabin fever and homeschooling, didn't seem unmanageable until my

Spouse started treatment for his drinking, after so many years of denial. Not to mention the

Surgery one of my lifelong friends needed for early stage breast cancer. And when my

Elder sister was diagnosed with cystic fibrosis at the age of fifty-two, this was a surprise to all of us. All in all, 2021 was filled with

Depression. My SAD (Seasonal Affective Disorder) hit an all-time low, and in October my husband was unexpectedly laid off from his job. But because I stayed on my meds, meditated, and used my Happy Light, I was able to plow through those winter blues. All in all, we are indeed BLESSED.

Acknowledgements

I would like to thank Alan Good for the time and care he put into the creation of this book. I will be forever indebted.

Thank you to the lovely professors I had at Hamline University. Deborah Keenan, Sheila O'Connor, Katrina Vandenberg, Angela Pelster-Weibe, and Laura Flynn are strong, brilliant women whom I deeply admire. Gorgeous writers, all.

Thank you to my writing pals: my readers, my friends, my confidants. You know who you are.

Thank you to Mitch and Jack. My home. My heart.

Thank you to the following publications and their editors for featuring earlier versions of my writing.

You're a High Flying Flag (*Open Minds Quarterly*)
Losing Her All Over Again (*Ellipsis Zine*)
Second Summer, originally published as "Indian Summer" (*Colorado Review*)
When My Mother Ironed (*North Dakota Quarterly*)
How to Activate Your Ancestry DNA (*Schuylkill Valley Journal*)
Greeting Cards (*Boston Literary Magazine*)
Snowball (*Anti Heroin Chic*)
Evening Out the Sides (*Pithead Chapel*)
Taming Your Prognosis (*Moonstone Arts Featured Poets Anthology*)
Color-by-Number, originally called Childhood Amnesia (*Bitchin Kitsch*)
Guess What's Different (*Red Fez*)
Sunburn (*North Dakota Quarterly*)
Snapshot at Gatorland (*Stepping Stones Magazine*)
Interwoven Foliage (*Schuylkill Valley Journal*)
Names Have Been Changed (*Serotonin*)
Explosive Orchids (*Schuylkill Valley Journal*)
Button-stitch, originally called Eyelet (*Red Fez*)
Matryoshka Dolls (*Cheat River Review*)

Susan holds an MA in Education and an MFA from Hamline University in St. Paul, MN, and has taught grades six through undergrad. Nominated for a Pushcart, Best of the Net, and Best Microfiction, her work will appear in the 2022 Best Microfiction Anthology. She is assistant nonfiction editor at *Pithead Chapel* and *Red Fez*. She lives in St. Paul with her family. You can find her work at susantriemert.com

9 781087 934709